CHANGING OUR FOOD

CHANGING OUR SELVES

CHANGING OUR FOOD

CHANGING OUR SELVES

Women, Food, Relationships & Culture

KAREN BURKE

HAZELDEN®

Hazelden
Center City, Minnesota 55012-0176

©1995 by Hazelden Foundation
All rights reserved. Published 1995
Printed in the United States of America
No portion of this publication may be
reproduced in any manner without the
written permission of the publisher

Library of Congress Cataloging-in-Publication Data
Burke, Karen, 1952-
    Changing our food, changing our selves : women, food, relationships,
and culture / Karen Burke.
        p. cm.
    Includes bibliographical references.
    ISBN 1-56838-096-8
    1. Women—Nutrition—Psychological aspects. 2. Women—Nutrition—
Social Aspects. I. Title.
TX361.W55B87 1995
613.2' 082–dc20   95-22168
                                                                              CIP

Editor's note
Hazelden offers a variety of information on chemical dependency and related
areas. Our publications do not necessarily represent Hazelden's programs, nor
do they officially speak for any Twelve Step organization.
    The following publishers have generously given permission to use quota-
tions from copyrighted works: From *God Makes the Rivers to Flow* by Eknath
Easwaran, copyright 1991. Reprinted by permission of Nilgiri Press, Tomales,
CA 94971. From *The Human Mind* by Karl Menninger, copyright 1964.
Reprinted by permission of Connie Menninger. From *Women Who Run with the
Wolves* by Clarissa Pinkola Estés, Ph.D., copyright 1992. Reprinted by permis-
sion of the author.

*As I look back on what I have written, I can
see that the very persons who have taken away my time
are those who have given me something to say.*
—KATHERINE PATERSON
THE SPYING HEART

To my family, Craig, Schuyler, and Aurora:
for you, with you, and because of you
there is always more.

and

To all those who have walked this path with me,
especially the Courage to Change group,
who give me just that.

Contents

Acknowledgments

Because my first step was a leap for me, I want to take this opportunity to thank those who leapt with me at this book's beginning and honor those people who so honored me.

I thank Timothy McIndoo, my endlessly skilled and sensitive editor, my artistic champion, my trusted friend. You believed in this book from the beginning and, in days of doubt, continually gave me back to myself. Without you I would be far poorer in spirit and this book would not exist.

I thank my husband, Craig Ayers, who, without commentary, attended to our children while I wrote this book; who listened to me talk about the process of writing it, listened and listened; who assented to my computer, my studio, and my writing schedule in consummate confidence. No wonder I married you.

I thank my mother, Katherine Benoit, who immediately understood, ratified, and substantiated my concept for this book. At a crucial time of hesitation, your resounding yes delivered me.

I thank my friend Patricia Ruble, who sat with me as sunlight turned to darkness that summer evening, while, oblivious of time, we percolated ideas that began this book. You listened in that joyous, active, soul-engaging way that only you can listen, and through your response made my direction real.

Finally, I am happily indebted to Stephen Mitchell and his translation of Lao Tzu's *Tao Te Ching,* which, though quoted directly only once in these pages, has given me a framework for my experiences, deepened and expanded my sense of the Eternal, and shown me a way to describe the indescribable, name the unnamable.

In ancient India lived a sculptor renowned for his life-sized statues of elephants. With trunks curled high, tusks thrust forward, thick legs trampling the earth, these carved beasts seemed to trumpet to the sky. One day, a king came to see these magnificent works and to commission statuary for his palace. Struck with wonder, he asked the sculptor, "What is the secret of your artistry?"

The sculptor quietly took his measure of the monarch and replied, "Great king, when, with the aid of many men, I quarry a gigantic piece of granite from the banks of the river, I have it set here in my courtyard. For a long time I do nothing but observe this block of stone and study it from every angle. I focus all my concentration on this task and won't allow anything or anybody to disturb me. At first, I see nothing but a huge and shapeless rock sitting there, meaningless, indifferent to my purposes, utterly out of place. It seems faintly resentful at having been dragged from its cool place by the rushing waters. Then, slowly, very slowly, I begin to notice something in the substance of the rock. I feel a presentiment . . . an outline, scarcely discernible, shows itself to me, though others, I suspect, would perceive nothing. I watch with an open eye and a joyous, eager heart. The outline grows stronger. Oh, yes, I can see it! An elephant is stirring in there!

"Only then do I start to work. For days flowing into weeks, I use my chisel and mallet, always clinging to my sense of that outline, which grows ever stronger. How the big fellow strains! How he yearns to be out! How he wants to live! It seems so clear to me now, for I know the one thing I must do: with utter singleness of purpose, I must chip away every last bit of stone that is not elephant. What then remains will be, must be, elephant."

—EKNATH EASWARAN
GOD MAKES THE RIVERS TO FLOW

The Dilemma

Food, the Four-Letter Word

Is there a topic among women more popular and yet more despised than food? Never mind that it's essential to our bodies, but terrorizes our spirits; never mind that we rarely feel so utterly ruined in the face of "self-improvement." Food is a woman's four-letter word: always fascinating; often guilt-evoking; often a source of shared pleasure, secret pleasure, and secret pain. Because in our culture we know such pressure to conform to a physical ideal, food also has the aura of the forbidden. We know that the pressure to achieve physical perfection is far greater for us as women than for men. Railing against that injustice is one of our favorite wastes of time.

It's a waste of time because it takes precious energy away from our inner directives, our internal calling to nourish ourselves as our bodies direct us when we really listen to them. The more heavily invested we are in the way our culture views our bodies (whether we're rebelling against that view or clinging to it), the more difficult it is to hear our personal directives of body and spirit.

The Food Change You Want to Make

A desire to change your food may mean a number of things. It may or may not translate into a weight issue. Maybe you want to quit eating sugar or drinking coffee or eating meat. Maybe you've developed a food allergy. Maybe you want to start observing a religious practice that involves specific foods. Maybe you want to eat at times other than traditional mealtimes, or maybe you simply want food to have a different place in your life.

When we get a call to change, we often push it back down before we have really listened to it. Why? Because it is uncomfortable and because we are afraid to fail. It's far more comfortable to hang on to our righteous anger about the impossible expectations on women and food in America, whether the expectation is coming from Martha Stewart or Susan Powter or *Playboy* magazine or Calvin Klein.

Every so often, though, many of us do earnestly try to make food changes. Something sparks us and we begin with great resolve. Often we do well for a time. Then what happens? We get busy, frustrated, tired; we get complaints from family members; we feel deprived. "I guess I just don't have what it takes after all," we conclude, and we give up. Until the next time.

If you are a woman, particularly a woman with a family, and if you have determined that you need to change something—anything—about the way you eat, it's likely you've found yourself swimming upstream. We get media advice on food until we're so full of it, it's like filling up on appetizers by mistake. Then comes the main course of living our lives, and we find ourselves full of something that doesn't fuel us for the long haul. We try to make our eating change stick, but often the change makes our food too different for the comfort of those around us or for ourselves. The change feels "out in left field" to our families, colleagues, and friends, and pretty soon to us too. What's the use? We think *maybe our resolve, crisp as a snow angel when new, was, like the snow angel, only a surface impression after all.* We think perhaps our food change was never meant to last. And we let our resolve melt away, a snow angel in the sun that leaves no trace but dirty puddles of guilt.

Our Triangle

We as women know our inherited version of the golden rule: feed unto others before you feed unto yourself. No matter how we operate in our own families now, the expectation to feed others first was built into our understanding of what a woman is. Like the fairy tale *The Princess and the Pea*, this expectation is the nugget under twenty mattresses of self-empowerment that keeps us tossing and turning.

Women have redefined their roles in many ways, but the vast majority of us are still responsible for buying groceries, providing meals, and making sure everyone is satisfied. The food gurus we read about in books and magazines or listen to on talk shows—who are often men and often people who aren't providing food for others—rarely take this into account. They act as if we have an independent, one-on-one relationship with food. But we don't. We have a triangular relationship:

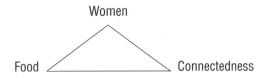

Thrust upon us is the role of the nurturing half of the species. We know it, and to some extent all of us live it. We nurture through connectedness and through food—often a combination of the two so interwoven that even we have a hard time sorting it out. (Try sorting it out with a newborn baby!)

When we change our own food, what happens to the connectedness, the feeling of relationship? What is the impact of the change on others? The dynamic within the triangle shifts. And what will help us with that shift? What will give us a picture of the dynamic on the other side of change?

That is the subject of this book. If you're trying to make a change in the food you eat, and if you have a family of your own or live with others, this book is for you. If you are expected to provide food for those others, this book is for you. It's the book I wish I had when I began to act on my inner directives about food.

CHAPTER 1

A Call to Change

My Food Changes

From my early teens to my early thirties, the way I lived in the world of food made me miserable. The shadow it cast was deeper, longer, wider, bigger than my own growing body—bigger than anything I felt I could do about it. Still, all the while I wanted a different relationship with food.

My first calling was to become a vegetarian. It bothered me to eat flesh, and I never really enjoyed the taste of any type of meat. But I didn't like many vegetables either, and everyone around me ate meat. Growing up I was told I was overweight in part because I didn't eat enough meat. Only my own inner directive was telling me that vegetarianism would be a positive change that would bring me closer to who I really was.

Once I became a vegetarian, my second calling was to shed my layers of protective fat. Overeating was my compulsion, and I couldn't see any way out of that behavior or any way to give up permanent residence in what my husband calls "The Land of Snacks." Most of the people I was closest to "pigged out" on a regular basis, in sadness and celebration, or just because it was Sunday afternoon. But inside I knew that fat wasn't the only price I paid for bingeing and that pigging out caused me far more distress than it ever relieved. So I began to address my food compulsion.

Once I began to heed this second call, I heard about people who had quit eating sugar, and something deep within me responded. Quitting sugar was a third inner directive. Yet I could hardly imagine anything more extreme. To me, people who quit eating sugar had to be saints or purists, Ghandis in training. Though I felt called to make this change, the only way I could imagine making it was to rig myself up to a permanent feeding tube. And I might as well be tube-fed, because *no sugar* spelled the end of pleasure for me. I didn't want to quit eating sugar, but I wanted to be free of my need for it, a need that controlled and contorted all my days.

One by one, I did find ways to honor each of those calls to change. Though no one I knew at the time was making the food changes I wanted to make, I ferreted out possible supports, discovered new friends, and worked hard to learn how they lived their lives so that I could change too.

But each time I made a change, my connectedness to one or several people in my life became threatened. I was afraid of alienating people with my resolves and of being too different from them. What would my partner think? My mother? My friends? My co-workers? Should I try to win my husband over to my new ways of eating, or were we destined to have separate meals for the rest of our lives? And if we always ate differently, what would that do to our relationship? What kind of food would I provide to others? What if I couldn't endure the temptation of their food, but nobody else liked my food? What kind of meals would I make?

Your Call to Change

You may be feeling an inner directive to make some of the same changes I did. Or perhaps you get sick every time you eat dairy food but find it impossible to avoid. Maybe your sinuses feel as if they've been stuffed with packing peanuts every time you eat wheat, but you find it's just too hard to take out of your diet. Or you've turned up with high cholesterol levels and your whole family is hooked on salty, buttered popcorn. Perhaps you need to tighten the family food budget, and you've become uncomfortably aware of how much soda or coffee your family guzzles, and how you lead the pack. Or maybe you're just tired of food-centered celebrations, tired of feeling bloated, worn out, and disgusted with yourself between Thanksgiving and New Year's, but once again all your relatives are looking forward to the traditional spreads.

Perhaps you've tried to make your food change before. Many societal messages push us to change. We hear advice on television, see the latest ads for diet centers, read the latest studies on the effects of caffeine, fat, salt, sugar, cholesterol. But the advice rarely addresses us in the context of our lives with our families. Without that context, it's just information without application, knowledge without wisdom.

How do we make a lasting change in the midst of the pressures of our lives? What about the desire to have the food we want in all those moments of tiredness and discouragement? What about tradition? What about the impact of our change on family togetherness? Is our food change worth creating dissension? And if we manage a personal change but our family members still eat the way they always did, it's painful to feel different from them. We don't like it. They don't like it. Who can live with constant deprivation when no one else under our own roof does?

The Meaning of a Call to Change

If you have an inner directive to change, chances are it will not go away. We hear the term "having a call" used when people talk about wanting to enter the ministry or become an artist. But is "call" too lofty a term for wanting to reform the way we nourish ourselves? I believe that a call to change our food is as divinely inspired, sacred, and creative as any inner drive we'll ever have.

But even as the topic of women and food has become sensationalized and pathologized, it has also become trivialized. The topic is trivialized because, in the end, we don't really think it's important—surely not as important as feeding our families and engineering family togetherness. We tend to tell ourselves that it's just vanity to want that food change, and our own lack of willpower is the reason we haven't made it. It's precisely because it is trivialized that the topic of women and food has become so tiresome. As women, it is considered our vital accomplishment to have a perfectly slender exterior, but we are not taught to give importance to our own inner directives about our bodies' nourishment. No wonder a call to change is so easily drowned out by society's expectations.

And it seems no woman is exempt from this expectation. I remember seeing Gloria Steinem at a speaking engagement, talking about her recent high school reunion. She said throngs of women gathered around her at the reunion—but not to renew old ties, hear about people she'd met, travels she made, or experiences she had as the seminal figure of the most sweeping social movement of our time. What all the women wanted to know was, "How do you stay so thin?" She said to her audience *sotto voce,* "They don't know I'm almost always hungry." We don't wonder why Gloria Steinem is starving herself; we *know* why. Even she has to conform to the standard. As a female public figure, Steinem has more power if she is thin.

We tend to respond to stories of famous people by feeling "less than." We tell ourselves, *Well of course she can stay thin; she can do anything—she's Gloria Steinem.* Or she's Oprah, with her personal chef, Cher with her personal trainer and twenty-two-year-old boyfriends. We know these women live in worlds different from our own. They are the goddesses! They can have all their food made for them and they don't have to make anyone else's food. We, on the other hand, are women with families and pressures and obligations and always more to do than there's time to do. That doesn't mean we let ourselves off the hook. It just means we tend to trivialize our own inner directives to change our food, if we hear those directives at all.

We are inclined to treat a calling like an impossible little-girl yearning to be a movie star: *Who am I kidding? I could never do that.*

Yet the call to change the way you nourish yourself is a vital part of your growth. It is deeply personal, deeply meaningful, and it comes from the center of who you are. And within the context of your life, your calling is possible to heed.

A Woman's Complex Path with Food

All my adult life I yearned for a different relationship with food from the one I grew up with, the one I took on. And where this calling led me has absolutely revolutionized my life. Now all these years later I have a different family configuration, different life's work, different ways of eating and approaching food—and the calling continues to revolutionize my life. My food changes have allowed me to love my body and to be at ease with its natural progressions through time; to become athletic in my own way; to have healthy pregnancies; to connect in new ways with those around me; to know the connection of body and soul.

When I changed what I ate, my attitude toward food changed as well. I became much more grateful for my food. I became mindful of how deeply symbolic food is. It took, and still takes, much internal footwork to make these changes stick and to listen for the rightful place of food in my life. But once I was committed to change, I found a lot of help. I looked for, and found, other men and women who were trying to make some of the same changes I was.

As I've listened to these people through the years, I've come to realize that a woman's path with food is highly complex in a way particular to women. We're the ones most often expected to provide the food, and yet we get the most pressure not to eat the food ourselves. I've seen many women begin their change with high hopes and then go home and find that the change upset their family dynamic, altered the power relationship between them and their partners, and made them feel alienated from everyone. So they quit, feeling worse than before they tried to change.

Why It Is So Hard to Change

Nothing can prepare us for how our attempts to change our food will affect the people we live with. That effect is sometimes massive, sometimes more subtle, but always seems to pack more of a wallop than we expect. We don't know what to do with others' reactions and with our reactions to their reactions. This is the unaddressed aspect of the topic of women and food, and it has driven many of us away from making the changes we want to make.

I think it's so difficult for us to make these changes because it upsets the triangle of women, food, and connectedness—a dynamic that is primal, so obvious that it can be hard to see. After all, women are almost certainly the first nourishment source for all of us, whether through the breast or the bottle. Throughout our formative years, most of us were fed almost solely by women. Our culture places a great premium on perfect women's bodies but at the same time has made women the designated feed bag. As women, we're comfortable with our purchase power at the grocery store, our power in the kitchen—a power we were trained to have. But our power to heed our call to change and upset our whole family dynamic as a result is a self-permission less easily granted.

Our food histories give us complications that, by and large, men are free of. We were taught as little girls that some day the legacy of food provider would be passed on to us—and not just food provider, but food experience provider. We understood what was expected of us by experiencing what was presented to us. We knew when we grew up, we wouldn't just make the meals; we would set the stage for them.

Reframing Our Food Histories

We all have food histories. Those memories affect how possible we perceive our change to be and how ambivalent we are about making it.

Many of us have particularly pleasing memories of our mother's baking. A friend of mine reminisced: "Baking was something I shared with my mother. I loved it when she'd start to bake and my brother and sister would be playing outside or in the living room. Mother knew why I hung around; and when the batter was mixed, she'd whisper, 'Wanna lick?' She'd take one beater from the mixer and hand me the other, and together we would lick them clean." The sweetness of batter was also the sweetness of connection with her mother in those moments of privilege, conspiracy, secrecy, and love. That little girl lives on inside the woman who today feels a terrible sense of loss at the idea of giving up sugar—even though she doesn't do much baking. And the secret way she consumes sugar today holds none of the delight her experience with her mother did.

I know a woman who converted from Christianity to Judaism in the last few years. She wants to deepen her faith by observing kosher dietary practices. Though she lives with a Jewish housemate and together they could cooperate to keep a kosher kitchen, she fears how making this food change would affect her relationship with her family and her Christian friends. She grew up in a close, devoted Lutheran family, full of memories of wonderful Easter and Christmas celebrations. It has taken time and understanding for her family to come to a degree of acceptance about her religious con-version. She fears the acceptance will dissolve if she eats according to kosher law, and her family members will be more alienated than ever. She doesn't know how to be with them if she doesn't eat the way they do, yet she does not want to compromise herself. She doesn't know how to resolve the conflict.

Another friend of mine had grandparents who immigrated from Switzerland before her mother was born. Foreign and tight-lipped, her grandmother had been a source of shame to her very American offspring; but in old age her characteristics took on an air of European mystery. When my friend's grandfather died, her grand-mother became the family matriarch, and all the children and grand-children would gather at her house every holiday. At those times her grandmother made a marvelous concoction, pastries whose recipe nobody knew. When someone would say, "Nana, what's in these?"

she would lift her chin and in her thick English declare, "None of your business!" So the family called them "none-of-your-businesses." They all derived identity and privilege from the knowledge that these pastries were their family tradition alone, their special treat. Years passed and the grandmother, growing more fragile, was finally ready to teach someone her secret recipe. *But no one wanted to learn it!* Every time they refused it was as though they were throwing charms at the feet of death. Somehow they all believed that if they never learned the pastry recipe, their grandmother would always be there to make it for them.

When the grandmother passed on, the pastries were not. Now a fading family legend, none-of-your-businesses are retired like a team retires the number of its great athlete. It's been many years since my friend's grandmother died, and many years since she tasted those pastries. But she can't let go of the ethos of the big holiday spread and the special baked goods she thinks she must make. This is true even though she doesn't enjoy baking, even though she's allergic to wheat but can't help eating what she bakes, even though it makes her sick.

Serving Food

There's something in us that wants to replicate what we knew. This may be reflected both in the type of food we think we have to serve or should be serving, and the authority with which we serve it. Patricia Hampl, in her memoir *A Romantic Education,* painted this scene:

> My grandmother, when she served dinner, was a virtuoso hanging on the edge of her own ecstatic performance. . . . She was a little power crazed: she had us, and, by God, we were going to eat. . . . The futility of saying no was supreme, and no one ever tried it. How could a son-in-law, already weakened near the point of imbecility by the once, twice, thrice charge to the barricade of pork and mashed potato, be expected to gather his feeble wit long enough to ignore the final call of his old commander when she sounded the alarm: "Pie, Fred?"

There wasn't much power to be had in society for many of our foremothers, but as the food source, they could take on a power that was hard to resist. Many of us experienced mother/daughter power struggles over food. A lot of us remember how guerrilla our resistance to our mother's feeding power became. At some point, and often as a matter of routine, our mothers forced us to eat food we didn't want. My friends and I have compared hilarious notes on the ways we foiled those watchful eyes. We poured food down the kitchen sink if she left the room. We fed it to the dog. We threw it in the bushes. We stuffed it down our clothes and into pockets, even the gooiest, most liquid rejects. All the while our mothers reigned, staunchly dedicated to the meal.

Our Role as Food Provider

As we contemplate our own food changes, it's helpful to look at the parallels between our mothers and ourselves as food providers. Many of them were home and had more time to plan and prepare meals. Today, the majority of us have outside jobs and are in a daily race against the clock. Many of our mothers had a prescribed monopoly on the kitchen, whether they actually wanted that or not; today many of us have partners helping with the meals, though the ultimate responsibility still usually falls to us. Most of us cannot do for our families what was done for us, and many of us don't want to. Still we carry patterns and expectations from our childhood, and they persist on some level as our measuring spoons.

Mealtimes, suppers particularly, have often been romanticized as a vehicle for communication, "proof" of close family ties—a standard constantly held up to us even today. As columnist Judith Martin says in *Miss Manners' Guide to the Turn of the Millennium,* "The dinner table is the center for the teaching and practicing not just of table manners but of conversation, consideration, tolerance, family feeling, and just about all the other accomplishments of polite society except the minuet."

Well, maybe. But these standards also provide some of the food baggage women carry. We're supposed to be gathering our family together; we're all supposed to be serving the same wonderfully nutritious food at the same time; we're supposed to be having a quintessential family experience.

How difficult it becomes, then, for us to declare any kind of independence with food; to eat at different times from our family; to quit eating a food our family loves; to quit providing a certain food for our family because we can't resist it. Change feels just plain wrong.

Our Covenants

When good change feels bad, it's time to think about our food covenants. In Christianity, a *covenant* is God's promise to care for us as we care for our God. It's an old-fashioned word. The word we're used to hearing to describe an agreement today is *contract*. It's significant that we say someone is *under contract* but use the phrase *enter into a covenant*. A covenant is not a contractual power of one entity over another but the coming onto sacred ground with a promise to one another.

We bring our memories and rituals of the past into our current situation. So do our partners. And together, largely unspoken, largely through unconscious habit and history, we form a covenant with our partners, and they with us. The covenant begins to form during courtship days, when we first engage in the intimacy of feeding one another. By the time we're feeding each other wedding cake, much of the unspoken covenant is in place. As couples continue to form a structure together, each woman brings with her the ghosts of past rituals, as does each partner. What we liked and didn't like about those early days becomes part of the definition of what is and is not acceptable now.

We come to some agreement on, though seldom verbalize, our food rules. Our covenants represent all the beliefs we have about eating, all the things we bring to food, all the things our partner brings, and whatever we may have taught our children to this point.

- When will we eat and what will that consist of?
- When do we eat together and when do we eat apart?
- Who cooks?
- What constitutes a "special meal" and when do we have them?
- What is a delicacy to each of us and when do we indulge in them?
- What do we teach our children about food and what disciplines do we have around it?
- What is the place of food in our lives?

When we begin to make a food change, our unspoken covenants need adjustment or reformation. If the change is large enough, it has the power to blow our covenants—and our relationships—completely apart. Sometimes we can see this before we even begin to make a change. But just as often, we realize for the first time what the rules are—our partners' or our own—only when we try to change them.

Our Blueprint for Change
Our challenge is to take all the elements, the joyful and the painful aspects of our food histories and current covenants, and mine them for gold, mine them for information about what does and does not feed us now. Then we can begin to make our calling legitimate to ourselves. We can explore ways to solidify our commitment to the change. We can consider the reactions we may get from the people closest to us and how we, in turn, can respond. We can examine our traditional role of food provider and consider which aspects of that role do and don't fit us now. Then we begin to see what change really means for us, what our calling to change is all about, what we get when we listen to it, and why no accomplishment is more important than this one.

CHAPTER 2

Fuel for The Inner Commitment

Sources of Change

We're all pretty well versed in the current societal messages about food. The things that are bad for us. The necessity to be thin and youthful looking. The magical something this week that constitutes the yellow brick road to clear skin, longer life, lower cholesterol, greater sexual desire, more energy. How do we sort out the external pressures from the calling within to make a change? How do we trace the source?

This is an essential question, because unless we know absolutely that we want to make a change *for our own sake,* we are simply being manipulated by the opinions around us about who and what we should be. It's a too-common female experience to be one step removed from ourselves, more trained in being desirable than desiring, more schooled in providing than achieving. How do we avoid all the expectations and "shoulds" around food choices, and discover what we really need? How do we know when a change is something we were called to make, not something thrust upon us?

Physical Cues

Physical cues are a blessing because they're unambiguous. If you're up all night every time you drink coffee after noon, you don't have to question what your body is telling you. A friend of mine finally quit eating dairy products because she got stomach pains so severe that she finally ended up in the emergency room. Another woman I know has become a vegetarian because eventually she couldn't keep down any meat she ate. Another can't have needed surgery until she loses weight. The good thing about physical cues is that you don't doubt yourself as much when you hear a wake-up call that borders on a scream.

If you consider yourself overweight, your struggle to listen to yourself could be more confusing because of the societal premium placed on female slenderness. Are you considered medically overweight? That may be a physical cue like the ones above. For others who are within a normal weight range but still consider themselves plump, it can be helpful to find out what other women weigh. I'm not referring to the weight on their driver's license, but to what they actually weigh. Ask women you know well, women who you think will answer honestly without taking offense. I am almost invariably surprised with what other women weigh; I tend to guess that every woman weighs less than she does—except me. Knowing the true statistics about others gives me perspective on my own statistics.

My Own Call to Lose Weight

Long before I ever sought out these yardsticks, I knew I was meant to weigh less—but not just because others let me know my size was unacceptable. I hated and feared and rebelled against what others thought, but that was not the worst part of being overweight. The deepest pain was the gut knowledge: *That is not me. That is not who I really am.*

I used food to cope with my feelings, but ironically I never could cope with my feelings as long as I used food in that way. I was never sure what my feelings were, because I tried to medicate them before I understood them. I was in a constant state of internal confusion. My inner directive was trying to tell me all along that my insides do not match my outsides.

I remember preparing for the wedding of an old family friend after I lost my excess weight. For my grandmother, I tried on the dress I was to wear to the wedding, and she was a runway audience unto herself. She gasped and clapped and bounced off her seat. "Oh Karen," she exclaimed, "aren't you glad now that you lost all that weight!"

"No, actually, I just finally feel like myself," I blurted. "I never did think that fat girl was *me!*" That was the first time I really knew the source of my pain.

All along I wanted glamour, sexiness, acceptability in society— the things that thinness promises and sometimes even delivers. But when I lost my excess weight, I didn't whoop for joy the way my grandmother did because I never identified with a heavy body. Becoming normal-sized was not so much a triumph over fat as a quiet relaxation. When I looked in the mirror, I finally recognized myself.

Our Heredity and Body Size

One way I knew I was distorting my natural body type was by looking at other members of my family. Since almost no one else was overweight, I knew my appearance was not dictated by heredity.

We all have a natural body type. The challenge is to accept it in the face of society's current conditioning. In the wonderful book on archetypal myth *Women Who Run with the Wolves,* Clarissa Pinkola Estés wrote the following:

> A friend and I once performed a tandem storytelling called 'Body Talk' about the ancestral blessings of our kith and kin. Opalanga is an African-American *griot,* and she is very tall, like a yew tree, and as slender. I am *una Mexicana,* and am built close to the ground and am of extravagant body. In addition to being mocked for being tall, as a child my friend was told that the split between her front teeth was the sign of being a liar. I was told that my body shape and size were the signs of being inferior and of having no self-control.

In this concurrent storytelling, on body, we spoke of the slings and arrows we received throughout our lives because, according to the great "they," our bodies were too much of this and not enough of that. In our telling, we sang a mourning song for the bodies we were not allowed to enjoy. . . .

How amazed I was to hear that as an adult she had journeyed to Gambia in West Africa and found some of her ancestral people, who, lo! had among their tribe many people who were very tall like the yew trees and as slender, and who had splits between their front teeth. This split, they explained to her, was called *Sakaya Yallah,* meaning 'opening of God'. . . it was understood as a sign of wisdom.

How surprised she was when I told her I had also as an adult journeyed to the isthmus of Tehuantepec in Mexico and found some of my ancestral people, who, lo! were a tribe with giant women who were strong, flirtatious, and commanding in this size. They had patted me . . . and plucked at me, boldly remarking that I was not quite fat enough. Did I eat enough? Had I been ill? I must try harder, they explained, for women are *La Tierra,* made round like the earth herself, for the earth holds so much. . . .

So in the performance, as in our lives, our personal stories, which began as experiences both oppressive and depressive, end with joy and a strong sense of self.

When we make a food change that involves our weight, we must consider our natural body type. Then we can make changes in accordance with, and out of love for, our natural bodies, however they are the same—and different—from others. This is one way we honor the temple of our body.

I've watched women use different methods to sort through this and come to love their natural bodies. One woman I know felt drawn to study karate; its discipline began to reshape both her body and her life. In working with her muscles, she came to realize her body had been a wider, less-toned version of her sister's—not a shorter, darker, factory-reject version of Cindy Crawford's. Though her sister's body was not model-perfect, she had always admired it. Now, through karate, she has come to recognize both her true physical self and her body's natural lineage.

Another friend of mine used her own history to answer the question of what is the right weight for her. She stopped reaching for a magical number on the scale that her body had never attained and instead pinpointed a time when she was at a comfortable, stable weight for at least a year or more. She chose as her new goal a weight that had proven to be a natural and achievable weight for her body, not a weight that was a temporary by-product of sickness, stress attacks, or newfound love.

Paying Attention to the Bodies of Other Women
If I relapse into mentally attacking my body, it's very helpful for me to put down the magazines and pay attention to *real women.*

I belong to a health club. I also take my children swimming at our community swimming pool. Both of these settings provide me with the opportunity to see women without the street clothing that disguises and breaks up the natural flow of their form. I'm reminded of the wide, natural, quite wonderful variance in women's bodies. I see that what we tend to label "disproportion" is in fact the real beauty that makes us all unique and interesting.

A close friend of mine works in a nursing home where she sees the natural progression of the aging process on women's bodies. She tells me about these aging characteristics and how she sees her own body changing gradually in the same way. Listening to her experience helps me keep a more humble, realistic perspective on my body as I age. As I approach any food change, it provides another opportunity to consider what is natural for my body in this stage of my life.

Take the time and use the tools you need to be clear about the food change you want to make. Assess the impact you think the change will have on your health, body size, and peace of mind. Consider whether the change you want to make will bring you closer to the person you are intended to become. These are sacred questions, soul questions about the care of your body. These questions deserve the consideration only you can give them, and their answers will bring you to your commitment.

The Loss That Comes with Change

As we solidify our commitment, it's both realistic and helpful to remind ourselves that all change has a price. Even when we make the most positive change, there is always loss. Recognizing it and expecting it is essential to staying on any path of change. Then when the going gets tough, we don't sabotage ourselves with, "I feel so bad, I guess I just wasn't meant to do this." We can be uncomfortable, sad, grouchy, or downright miserable and say, "This must be the loss that comes with the gain."

We may feel this loss initially or farther down the road. Often we feel it both places, in different forms. Know that these feelings aren't taking up permanent residence; they're just passing through.

Say you know for certain that it is time for a change with your food. You have convinced yourself, or your body or doctor has convinced you. You know what you must do. Maybe you've known it for a long time and, finally, *this is it*. Okay. But you are mad as hell. What to do? How to move through it? Let me give you a "for instance" out of my own recent experience.

Quitting a Habit

I was always very fond of soda, but once I quit eating sugar, I drank diet soda night and day. Usually it was noncaffeine soda; so for a long time it seemed like a pretty harmless pleasure. Wherever I went, all day long, all evening, I was usually accompanied by a can of soda. I had cartons of it at work. I brought it along on vacations. I loved getting it free at parties. If cans were left over from work conference refreshments, I would sneak an extra one or two to enjoy later. At home, I would forget I had a half-opened can somewhere and open up another one. I marveled at people who drank half a serving and threw the other half away. I liked it cold and fizzy of course, but when desperate I drank it warm or flat. I had my favorite brands, but if need be I'd guzzle any soda you offered me. The best restaurants for me were those that provided "bottomless" glasses, free refills, and I felt cheated by those that didn't. "Why couldn't they do for soda addicts what they do for coffee addicts?" I lamented.

I just threw the word *addict* in there for color. I didn't really think I was addicted. I knew I drank a lot of soda, but it seemed so harmless a habit that the word *addict* just didn't apply. And for most people, drinking soda is no problem. But in my case, the habit grew too large and began to carry too big a price tag.

Each hygienist who cleaned my teeth at my dental checkups would ask me if I drank a lot of coffee. I drank none, but they saw the same caramelly discoloration on my teeth that a coffee drinker has. Every checkup I clenched through the long, distasteful process of what they call *scaling*, scraping my teeth of stain.

Then a couple of years ago my dentist and hygienist told me I had the beginnings of gum disease. They said it was possibly reversible. They suggested trying to change the chemical climate of my mouth with meticulous cleaning and rinsing several times a day with prescription mouthwash. I asked what other factors might change the chemical climate of my mouth. Was there any correlation between drinking lots of diet soda and gum disease? Interesting question, they said. No research had been done.

I was secretly hoping they'd say, "Yes! Absolutely!" and then I would be forced once and for all to quit. I was actually disappointed when they didn't, because I was forced to listen to myself.

My inner directive wasn't interested in waiting for research. It said, "Quit. Now." It said my outsized consumption of soda was bad for my teeth, bad for my body. It said I was hooked and a better life awaited me without it.

For a long time I had felt uneasy about this habit. No one, with the possible exception of my spouse and a friend or two, drank as much soda as I did. My behavior with soda didn't match the other, healthier areas of my life. I was tired of wanting it, embarrassed to acknowledge I needed a daily supply. It was pleasure, but it was also captivity. And once I recognized it as a cage *around* me, it became "not me." Still I loved it so much, I didn't see how I could quit.

Then one day, shortly after my gum disease diagnosis, I woke up in a state of grace. It was one of those energetic mornings when the birds are singing and the sky is blue and everything seems possible. I got a very clear calling that day: *Quit! You can do it! As of today, you can be free!* So I heeded the call and quit drinking soda for three entire workdays without saying a word to anyone. Euphoria! That weekend I happened to go on a retreat and I did not bring a supply with me. There were soda vending machines but I left them alone. I was in a peaceful place, spiritually filled and out of my routine enough not to miss it.

Monday morning back at work I "hit the wall." I paced back and forth in my office. The morning was endless, the life ahead of me a flavorless savanna. Food was no fun without soda to wash it down. Yet I ate more food to compensate for the missing pleasure and the bite of soda. Water tasted horrible. There was nothing to do; nothing had the power to divert my attention from wanting it. At the same time I knew how bad I would feel if I took up the habit again.

Our Response to Loss

I was at that horrible place we all know when we try to quit something: I could not go back and I could not go forward.

That's the acute point of withdrawal and loss. What do we do? Do we hold on, bludgeon our way through; quit and go back to our habit; have a tantrum response? (One woman I know was so distressed at having to quit eating dairy foods, she went on a jelly bean binge for weeks. "Fine," she said, "if I can't have any of these foods I want, I'll just eat *anything*.") This place of rage and depression doesn't last, but while we are there, it seems to have no end.

We often dupe ourselves into believing that we would be having a different response if we were truly meant to change. We think we should be filled with happiness and self-congratulation. So we wonder what's wrong when we're angry, depressed, rebellious, looking for a fight. We may use the difficult feelings as "proof" that we shouldn't or can't make this change, even when another part of us wants this change "for good"—in all senses of the phrase.

(PS: I did quit drinking soda and my gum disease has abated.)

The Family's Role

Often at an angry and depressed point of loss, we turn to our loved ones and shriek, "Can't I get a little support around here?"

In my case, I thought to myself, *My spouse drinks soda all day long too. . . . Almost all my friends drink it. . . . My kids love it. . . . All my colleagues drink it. . . . It's everywhere I look. . . . This is impossible.*

And I was right. If I looked for support from people who are heavily and happily consuming what I'm trying to quit, I would be unlikely to get much help. And if I looked for support from people for whom soda holds no particular significance, they would have a hard time understanding how it could be a problem and would be unlikely to be of much help. Neither group could imagine why I would need to quit. Their conclusion: she's off the deep end.

Why Our Family Can't Help

Thinking our family can help is perhaps the mistake we make more often than any other. Like the country-western song "Looking for Love in All the Wrong Places," we often look for support in all the wrong places, foremost from our family. And if we don't get it from family members, we think we can't get it at all.

Albert Einstein said it is the theory we adopt that determines what can be observed. If your theory is, "I can't get support from my family, so I can't change," you may doom yourself to live in the discomfort of your unanswered call—a discomfort that often reveals itself in guilt, resentment, and shame.

The notion that you can't make a change without your family's support is a romanticized view of family life. The theory here goes,

"If they loved me, they would understand. They would agree with what I'm doing. They would help me do it." Believing this shifts our energy from making our own change to changing our family.

There are good reasons why this trap is so compelling. One is that it corroborates the notion that once our family sees we need to make a change, we will know it's really true. As long as our family is saying, "Well, I don't think you really have a problem," we may give that skepticism more weight than our own inner knowing. We can use that to talk ourselves out of change.

Or we may cling to the notion that our family's support will help us make our change. So we argue and insist upon certain behaviors and attitudes from family members about our change, when they may be totally baffled about what we're trying to do or may never agree that we should change. What an incredible burden we place on the people who love us!

Sometimes, yes, they may see us getting physically ill from a certain food. Then they believe, as we do, that a food change is warranted. Or they may have seen us miserable for years over the way we eat; maybe they even tried to get us to change before we wanted to. But often a change we want to make doesn't make sense to them. They don't see what we're doing now as a problem, so they don't understand our inner struggle. Or they think we hold impossibly high standards for ourselves. Or they think we've fallen under the influence of some strange cult or idea. Or they don't know what is motivating us. Our family sees what we do only some of the time and knows what it feels like inside our body none of the time.

"Neutralizing" Our Family

In the initial stages of commitment, the most helpful thing I know is to "neutralize" family members; that is, mentally place them in a position of neutrality about your change. Zap them all with a mental, comic-book-style neutralizer, whether you consider them supportive or not.

Even if your family outrightly sabotages your change, imagine for now that it is neutral. Even if your family members enthusiastically cheer you on, mentally fog them in a cloud of neutrality. From past experience you may be able to make pretty accurate guesses about their reactions. But mentally disarming them of all opinion will help you disengage. It will save you from counteractive, counterproductive rebellion. It will allow you to move into your commitment without taking what they say or do personally. For now, turn your attention in another direction.

Support from Our Like Kind
In my recent example, I wanted to quit drinking soda and I was at the crossroads of commitment. My years of experience with making food changes taught me that my family was not the appropriate place to look for support. But I was at the critical juncture, a point at which I had to have help or I could not move forward. Where could I turn? *I got my support by seeking my like kind.*

Two friends of mine had also quit drinking soda. One had become compulsive about it as I had; the other friend realized that Nutrasweet was causing her terrible headaches. I hadn't talked much with either of them about it, and they both had quit some time before. But their names came to my mind at the crucial time. (That's typical of the creative power I see people getting once they're really committed to change: names, places, sources of help come crawling out of their own mental woodwork. That's the kind of divine inspiration you'll get too.)

I called both these people the Monday morning I hit the wall. One of them answered. She became the first person I told that I was quitting. I hadn't wanted to declare myself to anyone before this, out of pride that I wanted to do it on my own and out of fear that I couldn't.

She heard me, understood my spot, validated what I was trying to do. She told me quitting was tough, she told me it was worth doing, and she told me I could do it. We talked about how I could get through that morning. We talked about how I could get through that afternoon. She told me when she would be available if I needed to call back. She understood that, as crazy as it might seem to others, I was at a crisis point of change.

Twelve Step Programs

My first, strongest, and most abiding source of like-kind support has been Overeaters Anonymous. I came into OA fourteen years ago, and it's not an exaggeration to say I owe much of the quality of my life to OA.

Overeaters Anonymous is based on the Twelve Steps of Alcoholics Anonymous, which suggest that we come to terms with our powerlessness, seek a spiritual foundation, write a personal inventory, make amends to those we've wronged, and develop a constant dedication to our own spirituality.

The Twelve Step program works for so many because it provides just enough scaffolding—just enough framework to build our own version of faith, however we start out, however we evolve, through however many changes and stages of life we go through. It gives a bare framework of exactly two hundred words. Not a book's worth, a chapter's worth, not even a single page's worth. Just two hundred words. Yet it is so complete a blueprint for change that it transforms life after life. And so simple. So free of lifestyle and life phases. So lacking in quarrel with any other kind of religion or nonreligion one might practice. So lacking in insistence that we believe any dogma at all. It simply says, If you want to move away from your problem, you must move toward who you really are. Here is a means of finding out who you really are. Millions have tried it, and millions have found that when they work for it, it works for them. I am one of those millions.

The night before I began writing this book, I had a powerful dream. In the dream I was staying at a hotel. I peeked out of my room and saw one of the founding members of my OA group checking into the same hotel. I knew she had seen me. I knew when she was done checking in, she would come and say hello. So I began to straighten up my room, arranging pillows and stuffed animals in pleasing groupings, while I prepared for bed. I heard a knock on the door, and in walked not one, but three members from my first group. These three were "founding mothers" who had shown me the way out of my compulsive overeating all those years ago. They spoke at length about what they saw in the relationship between me and my children, with many words of encouragement about my connection to them.

When I woke up, it was clear to me that these women were not talking about my biological children, but about the "children" of my recovery: the speeches I've made through the years, the things I've written, the friends I've made in the program, the people I've sponsored. It was one of those dreams so crystalline, so coherent, it was more like a visitation than a dream. Its gift was the affirmation it gave me as I began to write.

OA has been a place not just to make food changes, but to get validation and encouragement for all kinds of risk taking. It's also provided me with the strongest sense of community I know. I remember watching the movie *The Big Chill*, which centers around a reunion of close college friends. I sighed, "I wish so much I'd had a group of friends like that when I was in college." My husband answered, "What are you talking about! You have that *now!*" I realized he was right, that I have an abundance of community in my life, and I learned how to create that through belonging to OA.

The threads of my recovery are crisscrossed through many souls in the program, and theirs through mine. Many of us know each other well. We've laughed together, mourned together, fought together, celebrated together. We've stayed up all night keeping watch over one another. We've given each other shelter in the worst storms of our lives.

It isn't a perfect organization—it isn't organized at all. People come and go, sometimes painfully. The three women in my dream, for instance, are no longer active in OA. But we learned how to change our food together, and in the course of doing that, we changed our lives. We strengthened each other's commitment to change. In coming together weekly for our meetings, in talking together often on the phone, in breaking bread together, we came gradually to understand what we meant to one another. We learned to feed each other as we had never been fed before.

So although I haven't seen the women in my dream recently, their spirits continue to touch me with reminders of our connection. What they gave to me I try to give to others, and those people in turn give to someone else. Though the group configuration changes, a cosmic force of love and strength abides.

If your eating change can be addressed through a Twelve Step meeting, I cannot recommend it highly enough. If you've tried it before and it didn't work, try again. Look for a meeting with recovering people in regular attendance. Check out a variety of meetings to find a place where you are most at home. If you look, you will certainly find your like kind.

Other Means of Making New Connections

If you don't have a food compulsion, or if you are at odds with the recovery movement, you can get new support in other ways. You may think you don't know anyone who has done what you're trying to do. But once you begin to solidify your commitment to change and ask for support from God, the universe, the Great Spirit, or whatever divine source you are comfortable asking, you will be amazed to discover your change rising up to meet you. As the poet Goethe said, "The moment one definitely commits oneself, then Providence moves too."

The practice of any sort of prayer or meditation is a time-honored tool for "moving Providence." Don't hesitate to try it, however skeptically, even if you have no current spiritual practice or particular belief. It's amazing how a request made to any concept of the Divine can set off chain reactions, lucky breaks, and strange coincidences that will help you through.

And while you're making your request, talk to others about it. If you're comfortable doing so, discuss your food change with people at work. I have a colleague who had to quit eating wheat. By talking about it at work gatherings, she connected with a co-worker's spouse who has the same allergy.

If you have environmental allergies that require staying away from sprayed or chemically treated food, ask your health care provider how to contact others who have successfully made the transition you are trying to make.

If you are a trying to become a vegetarian, spend a little time at vegetarian restaurants and talk to the waitstaff, notice the people around you, start a conversation when you feel inspired to do so. If you would like to explore vegetarianism in a spiritual way, consider getting involved with the sects of Buddhism and Zen Buddhism that use this food practice as a part of their spiritual path. Getting involved will naturally introduce you to many others who have made the change.

Ask any friend or family member who feels safe—who you think will respect what you are trying to do—whether they know others who have made the same changes you're trying to make.

Go to the library and look for books about your food change. What suggestions do they offer for connecting with others in the same situation? (This is how I first found out about Overeaters Anonymous.)

If you feel safe and comfortable searching out others in your church, synagogue, or other spiritual circle, put up a notice, write something in the newsletter, or just ask around.

Trying these simple things will yield exciting results. The people you come in contact with may not turn out to be your closest friends—or they may—but they will do for you what your family may not be able to do at this point. It's impossible to foresee all the benefits you might derive from seeking out your like kind, but here are a few gifts you can receive from your like kind:

- They can talk about what it's like to walk in your shoes.
- They can listen to you talk about how hard it is.
- They can make suggestions about how to make it easier and tell you about things they did that worked.
- They can tell you how and why they made this change, and what it has meant for them.
- Above all, they can let you know that you are not alone.

Connecting with our like kind can help us make our change and reconfigure our own triangle of women, connectedness, and food. When we do something new with food, it makes sense to develop new sources of connectedness to help us rebalance our lives and absorb the change.

We need the new connections to help us understand both the change in our food and the change in our selves. We need a place to talk about our new vulnerability, to explore the ways we find ourselves living differently because of the change. We need to hear others who have made the change tell us how they did it.

"Tell Me about Me"

Listening to others fulfills a basic desire, a desire we always have when we connect with anyone, or read any book, or watch any film. The desire is *tell me about me.* Our human longing is to unlock our own mysteries, and that desire is all the more urgent and poignant in the face of change. So when we find our like kind, our connection to ourselves becomes more profound.

When I think of this circle of support, the movie *My Dinner with Andre* comes to mind. The two protagonists, Wally and Andre, had been friends years before and had lost touch with each other. The film is about their meeting again. Over dinner they compare notes on the courses their lives have taken. Wally is consumed with the nuts and bolts of earning a living, paying his bills, struggling with his career. Andre, on the other hand, is passionately involved with experiencing the meaning of life. Toward the end of the movie, Andre says,

> I keep thinking that what we need is a new language, a language of the heart . . . some kind of language between people that is a new kind of poetry, that's the poetry of the dancing bee, that tells us where the honey is . . . and I think that in order to create that language, you're going to have to learn how you can go through a looking glass, into another kind of perception, where you have that sense of being united to all things, and suddenly you understand everything.

I've walked out of an OA meeting many times feeling united with everything. And though there's a lot we come to understand together, there's even more we acknowledge as mystery. Together we are more at ease with knowing what we know and with not knowing what we don't know. We make for each other the "poetry of the dancing bee." We're a constant reminder to each other of why our food change is important and what else is important and "where the honey is." This seems to be true even if we have only one thing, like a food change, in common. The two friends in *My Dinner with Andre* have markedly dissimilar ideas about love, death, art, self-fulfillment. Before the dinner, Wally talks about meeting Andre with an anxious sense of social obligation and a reluctance to be drawn back into connection with him, or any friend. "All I thought about was money," he says. After hours in the restaurant talking with Andre, his focus completely shifts:

> I treated myself to a taxi. I rode home through the city streets. There wasn't a street, there wasn't a building, that wasn't connected to some memory in my mind. There I was buying a suit with my father. . . . There I was having an ice-cream soda after school. . . . When I finally came in, Debbie was home from work, and I told her everything about my dinner with Andre.

So we may start out thinking, *I have nothing in common with this person. Nothing but this food allergy (or compulsion, or whatever).* That may be true, and still . . . still you discover a feeling of deeper connectedness to your own life. We allow ourselves to be taken out of ourselves into other people's stories and yet in the end, they "tell us about us." Then we begin to know the depth and meaning of our own path.

CHAPTER 3

Meeting External Resistance

The Effect of Our Food Change on Others

When I began trying to change my food, I thought what I needed was willpower, pure and simple. I worried about how others would react, but I didn't realize how their reactions would affect my ability to stick with my change. I didn't have a concept of the food triangle: the relationship of women, connectedness, and food. I persisted in approaching change as though it were between me and food alone, without the powerful role of others' reactions in my own self-sabotage.

Since I've begun making food changes, I see other women experiencing the same reactions I received from family and friends. Diet centers, Twelve Step programs, and nutrition books don't help us with this. What do we do when another's reaction to our change becomes a painful sticking place? What do we do when our role as food provider shifts and becomes confusing and more difficult?

Change Your Food, Change Your Family

Nothing prepares us for the impact of our food change on the family dynamic. Often we aren't aware that our change will involve family members, so when we receive a negative response from them, we find ourselves without any coping tools. Our tender new resolve can get trampled in the wake of others' discomfort. We often end up backing away from our change because we fear for our connections to those closest to us, even though we can't necessarily explain what we fear.

It is very helpful to be armed up front with this truth: *Change your food and you will change your family.* Know that this will happen, even if it is the last thing you intend. Even if you are determined that your family members will not be affected, they will experience your change and will shift in response. How can this be? It happens because the change makes both you and your family aware of rules none of you ever knew existed until you broke them. And once you start to break those rules, you will shift the whole dynamic within your group.

This point can be illustrated with a simple experiment. The next time you're in an elevator with several others, wait until the door closes. Then turn around and face the others in the elevator. I guarantee you that every one of those people will shift in reaction to your movement. No one will stand still in the face of your face. It's a bold example of breaking a rule no one thinks about: when in an elevator, everyone faces the door. It's startling to break the rule, even though our behavior in an elevator is so automatic we don't even recognize its rules.

Reactions to our food change may not be so discomforting, but they are always there. Whether we're accepting a new limitation or going in a new direction, we are saying, *I can no longer handle eating in this way.* We've done some sort of about-face. Then we present that new face to those around us, and everyone moves in response. Maybe your family shift will be subtle, maybe radical. But your family will always change when you change.

And that whole possibility can be very frightening. Mignon McLaughlin, a writer in the 1930s, said, "It's the most unhappy people who most fear change." I wish I had heard that when I began to make my changes. I would have been better prepared if I had expected the unhappiest people in my life to be the most resistant to what I was trying to do—because they were.

Let's look at a few areas of our lives and the resistance that may come out of these areas, and how we can make our changes anyway.

Resistance from Partners

When I first began going to Overeaters Anonymous, my partner at the time had no idea what I was doing. Our relationship was strained at that point. I believed it would be even more strained if he knew, and I was right. So I went to meetings on the sly, talked to OA members on the phone, and made up flimsy lies to hide what I was doing.

Finally my partner confronted me. He accused me of having an affair. In the face of this accusation I couldn't think of anything to do but confess going to OA. I was full of shame: shame that he would come to the conclusion he did; shame that I had lied about OA; shame that I had this food compulsion to such an extent that he would know I was forced to align myself with, as he put it, "a bunch of fat losers."

Unfortunately my confession wasn't reassuring to him. The fact is, my OA attendance had a lot in common with having an affair. I was readjusting my allegiance, redefining the balance of power, telling my innermost secrets to another, engaging in illicit activity. Going to OA had a feeling of betrayal about it, even to me.

By going to OA, I admitted a problem that my partner never really knew was mine. He was angry that I had broken our unspoken agreements about food. He didn't understand why I thought I needed someone else's—not his—help to make my food change. Because I suddenly had all the people at my meeting to help me and didn't need him in the same way, he no longer felt needed at all. He felt completely left out. The spiritual foundation of OA seemed highly suspect to him, and he was convinced I had fallen under the influence of a bizarre religious cult. He hated OA. He fought back. He sabotaged my changes every chance he got.

Spousal Sabotage

In those days abstinence (the corollary to alcoholic sobriety) was defined as a very regimented food plan: three meals a day, nothing in between, no sugar, no white flour, every morsel measured, one measured serving of each food group specified. (Thankfully OA is different today. Abstinence is recognized as a very individual definition based on personal needs and personal honesty.) It took all my courage to measure out those modest servings and to believe I could survive on them, one meal to the next.

Along came my partner, and for the first time ever proceeded to *eat off my plate.* Without permission or comment, he simply reached over and began to eat my carefully measured food. Rarely have I experienced such total, violent, helpless rage. The only thing I could think to do was to refuse to eat with him.

I continued to go to my meetings, but some punishment awaited me whenever I got home. He would withdraw, greet me with coldness or sarcasm, or become very busy with work and torpedo the plans we'd made together. I continued to call people in the group but only when he was gone, to minimize the strain between us. So I was still hiding; it seemed as though I had simply exchanged one secret life for another. My resentment grew.

I changed my tactics and began to make and receive those calls openly. I flaunted giving my OA friends the love and warmth I had withdrawn from my partner. I stayed at the meetings longer, went to more meetings, got together with these new friends at other times, and became more and more unavailable to him. We had had significant problems before, but changing my food was the catalyst that turned our life into one long power struggle.

Earlier, while in a relationship with a different man, I had decided I wanted to become a vegetarian. I was nervous about telling my partner what I was doing. He was a confirmed meat eater, as was all of my family and nearly everyone I knew. I had no reason to think he would like my food change. He didn't.

The day I told him about my resolve, we went out for fast food at lunch. Temporarily forgetting, I nodded assent when he put in our usual burger orders. Just as we were finishing our lunches, a triumphant grin spread across his face and he said, "See! I knew you couldn't live without meat!" He sat back, grinning and confident that he had made his point and that I would now give up the whole sorry idea of vegetarianism. His ploy had the opposite effect and I have never eaten meat since. Our power struggle escalated, and our relationship, which was already in crisis, did not survive.

Since then, I've heard countless stories of spousal backlash and sabotage. A food change has enough force to split apart a relationship, especially one that is worn and straining already. It's very helpful to realize this and not underestimate the power of our change. If I had understood that power initially, I would have approached my food changes and my partners with more awareness and respect.

Other Common Reactions from Partners

In addition to anger and sabotage, another common reaction from partners to food change is puzzlement. They may say, "I don't think you really need to change. I don't understand why you're doing this." There are at least two good reasons for this reaction. One is what I'd call a "delayed reaction time" in the way people see each other.

The longer we know each other, the more likely it is that we see each other as we were rather than as we are today. This is a gift in a number of ways. My mother still sees the shy, vulnerable, child-me, and I want someone in the world to understand me this way. Inside my middle-aged face my husband still sees the twenty-five-year-old he first knew. I still can see the faces of my newborns inside my school-age children.

When we look at people we've known for years, it's as though we're looking at the starlit sky. Many stars are six hundred to eight hundred light-years away; our closest star, Proxima Centauri, is 4.3 light-years away. We can look at Proxima Centauri and think we're seeing it in the present, but actually we're seeing it as it was 4.3 years ago. For the most part, the way the sky is at the time we're looking at it will always be unknown to us.

I think the same is true with our loved ones, perhaps most of all with a partner of long-standing. We think we know each other, but the history between us—the habits and agreements and rituals of life together—affects what we see. The history connects us but it can also distance us. So when we want to make a food change, our partner may miss the signs that say our change is imminent. Instead our partner sees us as we have been and resists the change. He may be frustrated, angry, or puzzled. He may keep repeating, "I don't get it." Maybe we can't fully explain because, in some ways, neither do we.

Our partner may also be puzzled by our change because often we don't talk about the change process. Lillian Hellman wrote in her play *Toys in the Attic,* "People change and forget to tell each other." This "forgetting" is all the more likely when we make a food change because food is such a loaded subject for women, so shot full of shame that we don't want to bring it up with our partner. Like sex, money, and death, our food behaviors are among our deepest taboos. I know I never adequately prepared the people I lived with for the changes I made. I hinted, but never openly discussed how miserable my food patterns and secrets were making me.

Why should your partner accept a puzzling change that feels like a chasm you've dug between the two of you? It pays to take this question very seriously and realize the impact of our food change from our partner's point of view. We are placing limits that have never been placed before. We are asserting an independence of body and spirit that can be very threatening to our partner and to our relationship, regardless of whether either of us is "feminist," "traditional," or anywhere in between. The balance of power in the relationship always shifts, and we become more powerful. *Not that we have power over our partner,* but we claim our own personal power in a new way. We become more powerful to ourselves because we're heeding our own inner directive, and both of us feel that change and respond.

Approaching Our Partner

How then do we approach our food change with our partner? It is helpful to do some internal footwork as you are putting your change into practice.

First of all, consider whether you are quitting a habit you both share. This kind of change can be hardest to broach with a partner, particularly if he's uncomfortable with the habit, too, but isn't ready to make a change himself. This situation often elicits the most defensiveness and the most sabotage from a partner, and it helps to be prepared for that.

Letting Go of Our Partner's Food Choices

If you think your partner should make the same change you're making, talk it out with others who share your food change until you can fully let go of that idea. Once you embrace the approach that this change is *only about you,* not about him, you will be much better prepared to make your change in a positive way. Trying to force our food change on our partner is a recipe for disaster.

If we expect acceptance from him about our food, we need to give him that same acceptance, whether we approve of his food habits or not. Following our own inner directives about food means that we must allow others to do the same. This can be very hard for women, especially those seriously worried about their spouse's health. I've heard many women worry aloud about their partner's health and describe attempts to manipulate his diet. Our traditional food provider role can sometimes be used to justify making his food our business, even though we want no corresponding interference from him.

This is one of the great side benefits of going through our process: we learn to let go of other people's food choices, first and foremost our partner's. We learn we can't ask for the kind of respect we want unless we give it. At the table we begin treating him the way we want to be treated.

What to Say to Our Partner

If you are having a hard time adjusting to your food change or making your commitment solid, you may want to say that to your partner. But you don't need to give a lot of explanation. If your partner is curious about what you're doing and what your motivations are, he will ask, and you can give as much information as you are comfortable giving.

When we offer a lot of unsolicited explanation about our food change, it can sound as though we are trying to make him change too. But we don't need him to change in order to make our change. If he is to make his own food change, he will make it in his own time, according to his own inner directive. Saying little honors both the God within us and the God within our partner.

It also helps to be aware that use of a strident voice can be *us* arguing with ourselves. We might say, "I'm trying to make him understand, but he doesn't want me to change!" when really it is *we* who do not understand ourselves, *we* who are ambivalent about the change. If we hear ourselves saying a lot about our change to our partner, especially in aggressive tones, it's a sign that we're caught in an internal argument.

But there is no need to push anything. Practice making your change without a word. Offer whatever explanation is comfortable only when and if you're asked. If your food change makes some restaurant dining restricted for you and your partner, or if the food you prepare will be different from his, you may need to say more. Still, a good rule of thumb is, the less said the better.

In this way, both you and your partner are clear that you aren't pushing a food agenda on him. You are centering your energies completely on your change without the distraction of explaining, justifying, or arguing with another. You are better able to hear your own calling and heed it when you are quiet. And saying little will help mitigate negative reactions from your partner about your food change, because there is nothing verbally hostile for your partner to fight against.

However, your partner may express a lingering sadness about your change, even though he accepts it. As women, we're very susceptible to his sadness because of our food triangle; the food change threatens our connectedness to him. "He loved it when we went out for ice cream together, and he's disappointed that I don't eat ice cream anymore," one friend told me. "It's something special we used to do together, and I think he's just sad that I don't do that with him now." When we hear him express sadness, it's easy to feel guilty and fearful. He doesn't necessarily express this sadness to manipulate us. He may simply miss the food connection that is powerful for us all. If we feel deprived and teetery about our food change anyway, our partner's sadness can be just the rationale we need to declare our change impossible to sustain.

We can support him and ourselves best by hearing his reactions impersonally. We can observe what he says and does, and know that his feelings are his. We don't have to feel his feelings along with him, react to them, or declare responsibility for them. We can listen compassionately. When we practice this to the best of our ability, we make a great contribution to his adjustment and to our own change.

Our Partner's Adjustment
Often couples naturally develop compensatory rituals to replace the food connections. Perhaps they stop eating the same food together and in the process develop other independent behaviors that feed the relationship by giving it more "air." Perhaps they stop eating food at the same time but decide on a "date" once a week when they do eat together, and then they pay more attention to the mealtime together because it's special.

I believe our partner fully adjusts to our food change when he can see the new configuration—which, again like Proxima Centauri in the starlit sky, may be some time after you have made your change. When he is secure about his place in your change, he will relax. But that is not information you can give him ahead of time. You both must wait for the new configuration to settle in. Sometimes a partner ends up making the same change; sometimes it drives him deeper into the food you've given up; sometimes there seems to be no corresponding food change for him. But chances are you will see changes in your relationship in other ways. A partner's reaction can start out hostile, puzzled, or disbelieving, and you can continue to make your change, knowing that he may go through a number of reactions, just as you probably went through a number of changes to come to your commitment. Give him, and yourself, plenty of time.

The mutual respect that can develop between two people once the rearrangement is in place is surprising. Relationships often benefit from the constant practice of never commenting on, and thus always accepting, each other's food choices. Gifts of food to one another can become more meaningful than they have ever been, as they become signs of acceptance of each other's differences. We can eat differently from one another and the change can intensify the desire to give each other what we want and need. Paradoxically, autonomy deepens the bond.

Resistance from Children

Nowhere is the food triangle more vividly at work than with our children. The women/connectedness/food relationship begins before they are born because our bodies are their sole source of nourishment. If we breastfeed once they're born, our bodies continue to be their sole source of nourishment. We make our most powerful connection to our newborn babies by feeding them. Through food we establish their basis of survival, trust, and love.

Though others feed our children as time goes on, we usually remain their primary food provider. Even when our children are grown, we often continue to feed them on special occasions or at other times as an offering of support and love.

I've known many women who tried to make food changes and saw their children as a great stumbling block to those changes because of the things they think they must provide for them. We were raised with the conviction that mothers must give to their children. If we have needs, we must hold them in abeyance, subjugate them, fulfill them only if we can assure ourselves our children will not lose anything.

Deferring to Our Children

Because so many of us work outside the home and many of our own mothers did not, typically we have nowhere near the kind of time our mothers had to devote to the family. Yet we often expect ourselves to do for our children all that was done for us and more—it seems the standards of nurturance continually rise. As Lisa Alther wrote in her novel *Kin-Flicks,* "When she had been a child, children were expected to defer to their parents in everything, to wait on them and help around the house and so on; but when she became a parent and was ready to enjoy her turn at being deferred, the winds of fashion in child rearing had changed, and parents were expected to defer to their children in hopes of not squelching their imagination and creativity. She had missed out all the way around."

Many of us defer constantly to our children in the food arena; few of us are comfortable saying what was said to us growing up: "We're having meat loaf. Too bad. Eat it." That same deference leads us to believe that we can't banish certain foods from the house if our children love those foods. We don't want anything interfering with their positive food experiences. The more negative our own childhood food experiences, the more this is true.

So we persist in providing them what we think we should, even when it consistently goes against our own needs. Sometimes we're embarrassed to tell them we can't handle having certain foods in the house. Sometimes we fear a wedge coming between us and our children if we do not eat their birthday cake, put on big family feasts, or create sweet memories of them baking with us.

Yet in all the years I've talked to other women about food, I have never heard of a child attempting to sabotage the food change of her or his mother. Partners, absolutely! Parents, frequently! Friends, often! But children? Never. Children may occasionally offer us the foods we've quit eating, but unlike many adults, they always take no for an answer. They truly accept our refusal without taking it as a personal rejection.

The resistance we feel about our food change may come not from the children themselves but from our own ideas of motherhood. Anaïs Nin, perhaps the most famous diarist of the twentieth century, wrote, "Is devotion to others a cover for the hungers and needs of the self, of which one is ashamed? I was always ashamed to take. So I gave. It was not a virtue. It was a disguise."

If we stick with a food change for any length of time, it becomes painfully obvious that children had been our convenient excuse in the past. We stop buying cookies and after a week of mild grumbling, their world spins on. We make ourselves a different meal from theirs and they are all but oblivious. We quit eating hot dogs and they don't care. We don't eat their birthday cake and still their birthday is complete. We ask them to make more and more of their own food because we find we can't be around it, and they learn to make more than we ever thought they could, happily independent.

We have to quit using them as our excuse for not making our change. We realize that the need to cater to their food desires has been grossly exaggerated within us and may have been about something else altogether.

Once I realized this, I gained the ability to occasionally take off my "mother hat" around food. Even at my children's tender ages of five and eight, we approach equality on the subject of our appetites and our bodies and our responsibilities to each. They were more ready for this kind of change than I was! And, as in so many areas of my life, it's clear to me that I have much to learn from them.

A Child's Approach to Food

When we make a food change, it's helpful to take time out to consider how we feed our children. The attitudes and beliefs we bring to feeding them are deeply entwined with the way we were fed and the way we feed ourselves today.

How remarkably free kids are with food! I watch them and I see every day what Marc David writes about in his book *Nourishing Wisdom:* "Children eat naturally and spontaneously, without fear and without concepts of what should or should not be eaten. They certainly have their preferences, but unlike adults they experience little guilt and make no judgments about the eating habits of others. Children eat because they enjoy eating." Within the structure of eating that I know is right for me, I try to emulate their attitude. And they have freed me many moments, many days, from my own narrowness and rigidity.

Still, I will never totally regain the child's innocence with food. I have "eaten of the apple of the Tree of Knowledge of Good and Evil." In some ways this is positive, because my food behaviors inform my life like nothing else does. I know when I am beating myself up; I know when I'm stressed; I know when I'm secure and insecure—all as a result of what and how I eat. That knowledge is hard-earned and I wouldn't trade it. But that total freedom from self-judgment that is a child's natural innocence with food is lost to me.

Who takes the child's innocence away? Mostly we do. Children don't think any food is "bad" until we tell them; they don't think any hunger at any time of day is "wrong" until we insist that it is: "Don't spoil your appetite, you'll never eat supper." They have no shame about what they eat until we shame them.

When We Feed Our Children

I never ate like others and I still don't. I don't just eat different foods, I eat at different times of the day. I do most or all of my eating fairly early in the day. But more than not eating meat, more than not eating sugar, honoring my body's natural appetite curve has been an ongoing struggle because it goes against our culture. In the mid-1950s nutritionist Adelle Davis advised people to "eat breakfast like a king, lunch like a prince, and dinner like a pauper." Though that advice has been quoted and its wisdom confirmed through research many times since, our culture remains geared to the opposite: many people skip breakfast, have lunch on the run, and eat their biggest meal in the evening. It seems almost every social event is geared around large, often late, dinners.

My son's appetite curve is opposite mine but like my mother's: he is seldom hungry in the morning, but his appetite increases as the day goes on. My daughter's appetite curve is like my own: she's ready for breakfast instantly and eats heartily through the early hours, and her appetite tapers through the day.

Growing up, I was never allowed to eat according to my natural appetite. Dinner was a command performance. Should I try to pattern my children after me? Or after societal expectations of the big dinner, so they're in the groove of what's expected? Or let them go their own way?

It isn't always easy, but I practice letting my children eat according to their own appetite. I feel as brave as Margaret Mead with her infant daughter when she decided to follow Dr. Spock's then-revolutionary idea of feeding the baby "on demand." Feeding on demand is a common practice now, but only for babies. As soon as possible we start forcing toddlers and preschoolers into the arbitrary three-meals-a-day scheme, when what they usually want is about eight small snacks scattered throughout. At our house we have meals, but they are loose, subject to appetite, and voluntary.

What We Feed Our Children

Because making food changes has made me sensitive to my own needs, I've adopted a policy that is even more revolutionary than letting my children eat when they want to: whenever possible, I also let them choose their own menu. Each meal I ask them what they prefer. My children, like most children, prefer very simple food, so what they want most is easy to prepare. When a dish they are fond of is more time consuming to make, I'll make a large batch of it on the weekend and reheat it throughout the week. My son and daughter rarely want the same thing for their meal, so I'm a short-order cook. Except for one simple rule—no dessert unless you've finished your main meal—they almost always get whatever they crave. This is my contribution toward preserving their innocence about food.

If you want to try this approach but fear "unsound" nutrition practices, consider how much the nutritional wisdom we grew up with helped us. No matter how much I was scolded, I never voluntarily ate a vegetable until I was far into adulthood. I had nowhere near a balanced diet growing up, despite my mother's best intentions.

In addition to this, "nutritional wisdom" changes all the time. The Woody Allen movie *Sleeper* did a memorable parody on this subject. The film's hero, Miles Monroe, is the owner of a health food store. Miles is frozen for two hundred years. When he is thawed out, his two doctors discuss his case:

"Has he requested anything?"

"Yes, he requested some things called wheat germ, organic honey, and tiger's milk."

"Oh yes, those were the charmed substances that some years ago were thought to contain life-preserving properties."

"You mean there was no deep fat? No steak, or cream pies? Or hot fudge?"

"Those were thought to be unhealthy, precisely the opposite of what we now know to be true."

"Incredible!"

This bit of movie satire seems outlandish, but is it? Consider the egg. When I was growing up, the egg was often touted as the perfect food. In the 1980s it went from perfection to a cholesterol disaster. Eggs were to be avoided at such costs that we actually created a whole new industry—all new foods of "simulated egg," cholesterol-free eggs, or egg whites alone to avoid the evils of yolks. But recently we've received word that the egg is not as bad as we once thought.

Meat is another good example. Growing up I was consistently told that I was overweight partly because I didn't eat enough meat. Now meats are known to be high in fat, and many people have cut down or eliminated their meat consumption.

Milk was also touted as an absolute essential, the epitome of healthy food, when I was growing up. "Every body needs milk" was the dairy advertising slogan. Not until the activist late sixties and early seventies was it acknowledged that a large percentage of African Americans and many others lack the enzyme to digest milk. Now we have conflicting reports: we should drink milk for its calcium and avoid milk for its fat.

My mother fed me what was thought to be nutritious at the time: red meat at almost every dinner; sugar-laden breakfast cereals; lunches of peanut butter and jelly on white bread, peaches packed in heavy syrup, potato chips, and cookies. How would that rate on a nutrition scale today? In retrospect, how will my children rate the food I give them?

My guess is that the prevailing dos and don'ts of nutrition will change many times in our lifetime. The body's wants and needs also change. Children do a good job of listening to their bodies if they are allowed to. What we consider healthy and essential now may later prove neither healthy nor essential, and may not suit their bodies. So I have found great freedom for my children and myself by letting them choose their food and by keeping my monitoring and judging to an absolute minimum.

Buying and Serving Our Children's Food

I'm often asked if I keep sweets in the house, and I do. I think I was fortunate because I quit eating sugar years before I had my first child, so my no-sugar habit was firmly established. Sugar in the house is no problem for me, nor is soda, nor is meat. An invisible wall stands between me and those foods, so I don't have a need to keep them out of my house.

But if you are just beginning to learn to live without the food that caused you problems, it may not be possible for you to serve that food to your children without eating it. If that is the case, by all means, invoke your purchase power and don't buy it.

This is our frequent sticking place: we think we can't stop buying a food without harming our children. We see ourselves as depriving them of something essential to happiness and well-being. And for the first week or two, they'll confirm that idea! But children are amazingly adaptable to these things. We think we have to have such-and-such in the house for them. But actually, the food is essential only to us. I've heard many women sheepishly confess disappointment when they ban a certain food from the house and their children take it in stride. Because we care so much about a particular food, we think they do too. But it's our investment, not theirs.

Remember, no matter how young your children are, no matter whether you work full-time, part-time, or not at all outside the home, your children are fed at times by other people. Older children even have the option of spending their own money to buy a particular food. If you can't have certain foods around the house, your children can get those foods at other times and places. *We do not have to provide any particular food.* We just think we do.

Nowadays if my children offer some of their ice-cream cone to me, my occasional feeling of regret is not about turning down the food, but about saying no in the face of their generosity. So I make sure to build in other moments of sweetness. I've reconstructed my food triangle with my children by creating many other connecting rituals with them, some of which revolve around food. (More about this in chapter 5.) As a family we don't usually sit down together and eat identical food. As you practice your change, your family meals may evolve like this or they may not. Either way, family closeness is still palpable—meaning, of course, you can taste it.

Resistance from Mothers

While swapping food stories with other women, I've discovered that the most common source of resistance to our food change, next to our partner, is our mother. Usually, our mother fed us from the start of our lives. And we may still feel obligated to explain our food change to her, even though we're adults with families of our own.

Our Mother's Investment in Our Food

Our mother may continue to take a keen interest in what we are putting in our mouths. She is often the only one who still cooks for us once we're grown. And her actual identity may be tied to the success of feeding us, because the role of food provider figures so largely in the role of mother. No wonder she is more likely than anyone to feel personally rejected if we reject her food.

With mothers, the triangle of women, connectedness, and food is potent and complex. We have to some extent shaped the very nature of our connection to her through the way we've received her food, whether appreciatively or rebelliously or indifferently. We've also absorbed the impact of myriad attitudes, skills, and ideas about food presentation through the way she handled the role of food provider. My mother disliked cooking as I was growing up, and I took on her dislike. Perhaps you had the opposite experience, and you've inherited your mother's love of cooking and her sense of its primacy in family life. Either way, a legacy passes between mother and daughter in the female role of food provider, and that history is bound to be reflected in her response to your food change.

When you were growing up, your mother probably decided what could and could not be bought at the grocery store. She decided when you had to share your treats with a sibling or a friend. She decided when you could leave the table and when you would have to sit in front of your mashed potatoes long after they were cold and the other family members had left to resume their evening. You knew what the rules were, the spoken ones and the unspoken ones, what food was deemed healthy and what was not. Perhaps you rebelled against much of what you were taught growing up. Or perhaps your current food change constitutes your first major rejection of your family's food covenant. Either way, it is likely that your mother will care about, and respond to, your change.

Our Responses to Our Mother

Your mother might have a reaction as benign as, "Help me understand," and "When you come, what food should I prepare instead?" Or her reaction might be, "Why are you being so difficult?" Maybe you imagine her muttering under her breath, "I wonder how long this kick is going to last!" Or was that not your imagination?

The best way I know to deal with a mother is with gentleness, whether she is gentle with us or not. Remember that you are shifting the food triangle in a powerful way: you are reforming the covenant with your original food provider, the person who most sought connection to you through food.

When I first turned down foods I had always accepted from my mother, it worked best when, in the very next breath, I affirmed our connection in another way. Calling her an affectionate nickname, referring to a happy memory or something we both find amusing, and complimenting her about something were ways of affirming our connection while refusing her food. Explanations of why I was changing my food habits didn't seem nearly so important as this affirmation.

As a matter of fact, giving unrequested detail about my change often made me hostile and defensive, and she would respond in kind. As a rule of thumb, if we find ourselves talking on and on about our reasons for our change, it's a good clue that we haven't quite reconciled ourselves to the change yet. If this happens we can go back to strengthening our commitment. We can get help from our like kind. The battle within is much better played out with the people who understand and support our change. Involving our mother to our battle doesn't help and can often cause a good deal of damage. Whether mothers are strict or lax, affirming or punishing, opinionated or reserved, they are seldom uninterested in their children.

It is important to realize that our mother is often vulnerable about what she fed and didn't feed us from conception. We did, after all, share the deepest intimacy, her very body; and her care of our nourishment was essential to her definition as mother. Our mother, like us, does the best she can with what she knows at the time.

Even if you don't believe she did the best with what she knew, still it does the least damage to her and to you to say as little as possible. If it is appropriate to actually "announce" a food change, we can do that without any reference to our mother or the past. Finger-pointing statements like, "I'm trying to reverse some of the damage you did to me growing up," or indictable comments like, "Why did you always buy those cookies when you knew I couldn't keep away from them?" or evangelistic approaches like, "Don't you realize what you're putting into your body when you eat meat?" bruise us all. Until we can approach our mother neutrally, however biased she may be, we are better off making no announcements. We can eat according to our food change and quietly decline anything we've decided against eating. When our mother notices the new pattern and asks about it, we will have taken the time we need to work through the conflicts of the past. Then we can answer in a way that keeps the topic just about us. When we do this, we help both our mother and ourselves adjust to the change.

Resistance from Fathers

Fathers usually react quite differently to our food change than mothers do. Because so few of them actually served our food, their investment in any changes we make as adults is usually much less. Their reactions often range from neutral to oblivious. A number of women I spoke with about their father's role in their food changes commented on the fact that their father will offer them a food they quit eating years ago. Their father was completely unaware they had changed their food, despite being told on any number of occasions.

If your father reacts strongly to your change, chances are that you also had to answer to him about your food while you were growing up. Then your change may be the declaration of independence so many of us experience with our mother.

But with fathers there can sometimes be the added layer of facing the fierce, all-knowing, ultimate authority. It's the voice that often gets confused with the male, external God of our culture: we cannot do anything significant without obtaining His permission. Writer Katherine Mansfield captured the feeling well when she wrote, "Josephine had had a moment of absolute terror at the cemetery, while the coffin was lowered, to think that she and Constantia had done this thing without asking his permission. What would father say when he found out? For he was bound to find out sooner or later. He always did. 'Buried. You two girls had me buried!'"

The sense that their father is the absolute, ever-watchful authority still permeates some women's lives. I have a friend who saw her mother reach for a dessert at a family gathering. Her father looked at her mother and charged, "Should you really be having that?" My friend could not get over it—her mother was eighty-two years old! When would her father quit watchdogging her mother's food? When would her mother be allowed to relax? When would her body ever be hers?

The challenge with fathers, like mothers, is deciding without rebellion who your ultimate authority will be. Is it your own inner guidance? Is it a health professional, one who convinced you to make a food change for your body's sake? Or is it your father or your mother? Or the version of your parents that you hold inside your head? Once we take the time to identify our ultimate authority for ourselves, the voice in our head becomes our adult desire to chart our own course: *I will make these changes for my health's sake.* Or perhaps the voice in our head gives rein to our more childlike impulses: *Wouldn't it be fun to have pizza for breakfast!* When we are clear about our ultimate authority, we are no longer ruled by a voice in our head that masquerades as our parents, that can scold and shame our desire to change.

Resistance from Other Women

What makes the topic of food so tough for women around other women?

I went on my first diet when I was thirteen. It began on a Saturday afternoon when I was shopping with my friend Linda and her mother and sister. Before we left the store, Linda's mother suggested chocolate ice-cream cones for us all. Count me in! But mysteriously, and for the first time in all the years I'd known her, Linda refused the ice-cream cone.

This I could not believe. Nor did Linda want to talk about it. But I felt I was within my rights to bully an answer out of her. After all, she'd just broken the rule we lived by: girls in their early teens can never deviate much from one another. It was safest to have the same eating habits, behaviors, interests, speech, clothes, and body size. I had another friend then who was petite while I was tall. We were ridiculed by our peers for hanging out together because of our size discrepancy. It took a certain amount of courage just to walk side by side down the hall at school.

Linda and I, on the other hand, were very comfortably the same size. Same height. *Same puppy-fat weight.* So what was she doing refusing an ice-cream cone? Was she sick?

Linda eventually gave in to my badgering and revealed that she was on *a diet*—a completely revolutionary idea in my young life! Then, of course, I had to be on a diet too. After all, I couldn't let her go on this adventure of suffering and glamour alone. So we proceeded on the most woefully inaccurate nutritional information (eat only a hot dog for lunch, which is "good" food, but skip the bun, which is "fattening"), starved exotically, and lost eighteen pounds in three weeks. I gained it back like a runaway train, and more, and more, and that was the real beginning of my problems with food.

Other Women's Reactions

When we first refuse a food, it's not unusual to be greeted, even by our best friends, with, "What's your problem? I don't get it." It's not unusual to be goaded with, "Trying to make me feel guilty, huh?" when a friend eats dessert and we do not. It's not unusual for a friend to martyr herself with an unhappy, "Well, if you're not having any, I guess I won't either." Within many of us lurks a thirteen-year-old who doesn't want her best friends looking too different from her.

Another common reaction among women is to canonize the friend who has made food changes: "Oh, you're such a *saint!* God, I wish I had your willpower." That's uncomfortable too. We know, and they know, that long-term change is not a question of "willpower." Eating is part of the whole life we choose, its shape and quality. That may be precisely why it can be so hard not to draw attention to our food around other women. They tend to be more aware of the significance of our food choices.

Recently my mother told me about an afternoon visit with her friend June. June was hell-bent on serving my mother a snack to show her hospitality. My mother didn't want the snack. She also needed to refuse the coffee, knowing it would keep her awake that night. But June would not give up. "Isn't there *anything* I can get you?" she lamented. The offers and refusals went on throughout the visit, and by the end my mother was sorry she had ever come.

Why do women put each other through this? I think the roots go deep, back to where we think our basic value lies. Maria Augusta Trapp, whose story became famous in the musical *The Sound of Music,* wrote, "But if one doesn't have a character like Abraham Lincoln or Joan of Arc, a diet simply disintegrates into eating exactly what you want to eat, but with a bad conscience." When it comes to food, lives there a woman without a bad conscience? And how that conscience is evoked when another woman turns down food! It seems to spark Eve's lament of original sin: "I want to have this 'forbidden' food. Come join me and relieve me of this guilt, so I don't have to feel like I've sinned."

Turning Down Another Woman's Food

How can we avoid making other women feel guilty when guilt is women's most readily available response to food? Again, I recommend the approach of great compassion and few words. You may want to explain to close friends the process behind your change. But with other women, often it isn't necessary or desirable to say anything.

If I am eating with a hostess and she offers me something, I've found three words, that for some reason, work better for me than any others: "I'm fine, thanks." I'm not sure why this phrase is more effective than saying, "No thank you." Perhaps the politeness of my *no* makes me sound less firm than I really am. Perhaps *no* leads more to speculation about why I am refusing. Maybe it's simply the free-floating agitation people can feel when they hear the word. So I never use *no* when I turn down food.

I use the phrase "I'm fine, thanks" as much for them as for me, because for me it evokes a sense of inner peace. It recalls for me the prayer of Saint Teresa of Avila:

> Let nothing disturb thee,
> Nothing dismay thee.
> All things pass;
> God never changes.
> He who has God, lacks nothing.
> God alone is sufficient.

When I say, "I'm fine, thanks," I am saying, "I feel complete, I am enjoying your company, I am relaxed, I am here, and I have everything I need." It may be, too, that the phrase invites an echoing sense of peace in others. My hope is that my gratitude comes through, and my hostess will know she needn't go on attempting to satisfy me. Whatever chord it strikes in other women, "I'm fine, thanks" almost always yields acceptance.

Resistance from the Work Environment

Work is one of those places where it usually pays to have a well-cultivated herd instinct. To a larger or smaller extent, our ability to fit into our work establishment guarantees our job.

The Meanings of Food in the Workplace

Food is one way to connect and fit in at work. We recognize that food is a need and a vulnerability we all share—without it, we all die. And eating together can go beyond hierarchical relationships to establish warmth and conviviality. It can lessen a sense of threat, heighten security, and remind us that we're all humans, working together side by side.

But even food has its politics. These days we have power breakfasts, power lunches. Magazine articles describe what to eat and not to eat at "power meals." And, of course, you're always a step ahead if you order what the boss ordered. My mother once worked for a company owned by Mormons. Many Mormons adhere to certain dietary practices, avoiding what they consider harmful substances as part of their religious practice. My mother soon found it was much more comfortable for her as an employee to switch from coffee to tea, margarine to butter, and otherwise eat as her bosses ate.

Eating with Colleagues

One of the most uncomfortable moments of my work life came when I was forced to be the recipient of a good-bye luncheon. I had been part of a team I was never comfortable with, and now I was being reassigned. My colleagues had seemed no more comfortable working with me than I was with them, and I think we were all glad I was moving on.

This group rarely socialized together. But taking departing colleagues to lunch was a norm; they didn't want to slight me. I in turn didn't want to slight them, knowing that I would need to continue working with them in other capacities. I don't think they wanted to take me out any more than I wanted to go, but no one could figure a graceful way out it. So we went, as was the custom, to the restaurant of my choice.

I unwittingly chose a health food restaurant where I realized—too late—the rest of them never went. As I watched them struggle with the menu, I remembered other times and places where I felt like an outcast. My restaurant choice personified everything that made me feel like a misfit while I worked with them. That lunch played out a keen and horrible sense of failure.

In the workplace, some of us are very comfortable around our colleagues and may count them among our dearest friends. Others of us work in a standoffish or hostile environment. But the workplace is rarely neutral. Why should it be, when we spend so many hours of our day there, when human beings are so varied and complex?

Some people try to forge a bridge through communal eating. It's typical to have a co-worker or two (is this *ever* a man?) with a candy jar, whose desk becomes a sort of alternate "watercooler" to gather around and chat throughout the day. Some workplaces have events throughout the year that include structured "eating together" time. Many of us have co-workers who constantly bring in "goodies" to share.

Changing Our Food in the Workplace

How do we handle our food changes in the workplace? We probably need to say much less than we think we do. To turn down food we know we can't handle, the magic phrase "I'm fine, thanks!" works well. We don't need to explain our food patterns. We may know we *never* eat those foods, but there's a surprising lack of need to pronounce it; in our co-workers' eyes, we can be turning it down just this time. Even if you work in a close-knit group that has alternated bringing treats to work, you needn't say much. You can gently bow out of the rotation with only as much explanation as you are comfortable giving.

I have gone through many stages with co-workers and food, and they mirror my stages of change. When I first began attending OA groups, it was important to me to keep my anonymity. I realized, too, that my spiritual approach to food would not be something I'd be comfortable talking about to everyone and not something everyone would feel comfortable listening to. As my food changes became habit and I had good feelings of accomplishment around them, I volunteered more information. But talking about it sometimes led to an unwelcome, "I could *never* be as good as you!" response from others, and then I'd feel painfully apart. Now I'm back to saying little yet striving for consideration of others as much as I can. For instance, if I had to be the recipient of a farewell luncheon today, I would make a concerted effort to find a restaurant where everyone would feel at home.

But this does not mean I give my own needs away to the comfort of others. I work with many vendors, and recently a sales representative wanted to give me a tour of his company and was adamant about treating me to lunch. I did not want to be taken to lunch. But instead of going into details about my food, I gave him an equally true explanation: "Thanks, but lunch is the only time of my day that is my true break. It doesn't belong to my work, my children, my spouse, my church, my community. It's my quiet time, and I maintain sanity by keeping it my own. But thanks for thinking of me." Even as a salesman schooled in the hard sell, he accepted that.

Separation of Work and Food
I believe in separation of work and food. I work closely with many people who are involved with providing much of the nation's or the region's food. I work with people involved with cattle, pork, and other meat industries as well as sugar growers. Through my work I

often help promote these products, and I do it without announcing that I eat none of these things.

I eat occasionally with co-workers, but never comment on their food. Every once in a while someone who knows my habits will ask, "Will it bother you if I eat this?" or "Are you still a vegetarian?" But none of it is a problem. Amazing how much easier it is to focus on my friend at her farewell party because I'm not waiting to go through the refreshment line. Amazing to know that whatever treat a co-worker might bring in does not have to trouble me if it's not part of what's right for my body. Amazing to see how easy it is to say, "I'm fine, thanks," with all graciousness. Amazing to remember how much I thought work situations were roadblocks to change, yet once I practiced my commitment, how little my coworkers noticed.

Talking About Our Change/ Not Talking About Our Change

This chapter suggests that we probably need to say much less than we think we do about our food change, regardless of where the resistance is coming from. But that doesn't mean never talking about our difficulties with our commitment or with practicing that commitment around other people. It just means choosing our forums well.

When we're disturbed about an external resistance, it's important to pay attention. The disturbance we feel has probably tapped a resistance within ourselves. We need to talk about our reactions in order to work through them and keep our commitment strong. We need to go back to our sources of support, our like kind, and discuss a disturbing situation at whatever length we need to. We will come to know what has bothered us, stopped us, kept us stuck, or kept us reacting. We can gather suggestions from our like kind about moving through such situations. We can examine our internal piece that was called by the external resistance—that piece of us that doesn't want to change.

With practice we become graceful with others, until no reaction from another feels like resistance. Then everything around and within us can be embraced, and we can move on.

CHAPTER 4

Moving Through Conflicts

Handling Others' Judgments of Us

My most helpful rule of thumb when moving through external conflicts is to *give up trying to be understood.* This is especially true in the very place we most want to be understood, within our own family.

Maybe your family members have seen your food problem, but maybe they don't have a clue. Especially if we have a food compulsion, we can hide our problem like the Most Wanted hide, with incredible cunning, terror, and sleight-of-hand. Those closest to me rarely saw me binge or reveal food obsessions because I was that tricky, that secretive. Nevertheless, when I gave up the jig, I felt hurt and misunderstood when my family responded with a collective, "Say *what?*" I was expecting my family members to understand the depth of my problem and the ways I needed to change, when they rarely witnessed that I *had* a problem.

Even if your family members know on some level why you're doing what you're doing with food, they may not really understand. Once we decide we want to change, we may think we need to convince our partner or other family members that we really do have a food problem. It's tempting to try to make them understand, and it can be just the excuse we've been looking for to abandon ourselves when they don't.

Psychiatrist Karl Menninger wrote about understanding one another in a way that touched me so profoundly, I taped his words to my bathroom cabinet. I read this as part of my routine preparation to meet my world, a kind of daily flossing between the ego cracks:

> When a trout rising to a fly gets hooked on a line and finds himself unable to swim about freely, he begins with a fight that results in struggles and splashes and sometimes an escape. Often, of course, the situation is too much for him.
>
> In the same way the human being struggles with his environment and with the hooks that catch him. Sometimes he masters his difficulties; sometimes they are too much for him. His struggles are all that the world sees and it naturally misunderstands them. It is hard for a free fish to understand what is happening to a hooked one.

Menninger's image reminds me that no one may fully understand my own "hooked" state. Others may see me flail, but even those closest to me cannot *know*, as long as they are free of my problem. And I mustn't expect them to know.

I am also reminded to hold my own judgments at bay, because likewise I can never totally know what hooks another person. Many people close to me have suffered food compulsions, or clearly need to make a food change for their health. Many have made their change and many have not. I can never know the hooks that keep people where they are. If they ask me how I made my changes, I can say, "This is what I did," and maybe they will try those things or follow other approaches that draw them. Maybe they will free themselves. But often, whether they seek outside help or not, their food problem is too much for them.

The image of the fish gives me a constant reminder of compassion for us all: to not lever the demand to be "understood"; to not expect that someone who loves me to have the magic power to unhook me; to help unhook the ones I can, if that's possible; to not expect results when I try to help; to not presume that I understand completely what is hooking me or them; and to swim in camaraderie alongside each other because none of us can see the hook coming.

Handling Our Judgments of Others

It follows that if I am to release myself of others' judgments about my food, I need to avoid judging anyone else's food. Because of women's traditional role as food provider, this can be one of the most difficult aspects of our change process.

When we change our food, we become more aware of our family's food. Perhaps we see in our partner a food compulsion or caffeine addiction. Perhaps we suspect a family member has a food allergy. Perhaps we see our children eating in ways we want to "fix." Perhaps the idea of eating meat now repels us, and yet the rest of our family wants it. As the main purchaser of food, the primary server of meals, how much do we try to get other family members to "clean up their act"?

I would say, "fix" as little and as gently as possible. To whatever extent I can, I keep food changes just about me. I work hard at not judging those I love and placing my food standards on them. My husband and my children have many foods in their diet I don't, including soda, sugar, gum, meats, and coffee. Yet I've created some family norms, as unobtrusively as I know how: whole wheat breads, nonfat milk, early no-big-deal suppers, limited dairy foods, dessert in its place, a certain amount of rotation of foods. These things I can do because I buy the foods. But I don't refuse to provide what they want, and I don't deliver lectures du jour. To whatever extent I can, I let my family members' own spirits and bodies guide them, as I expect them to let mine guide me.

Changing Our Food Provider Role

I've mentioned that I'm a "short-order cook" in my house, and my experience doesn't seem to be atypical. It seems that when a woman no longer eats like the rest of her family, everyone ends up with a different meal. When I get together with other women and talk about this, we all agree that if our partner had made the food change, the impact would not have been the same. We think it's more likely that the whole family would start to eat more like our partner, to simplify matters for us as the cook. We're guessing that a food change of his would not necessarily change our role as food provider; it would only change what we provide.

But when we're the ones changing, we loosen our hold on the role of food provider. We teach our children how to prepare their food earlier in life. We encourage, or are relaxed with, our partner getting his own food if he didn't before. And the gradual evolution seems to be that we all do our own thing. Often the family members eat at different times that suit each of them; other times they eat together, but eat different food.

It's a paradox: the more we keep a good boundary on our food change, keeping it confined to what is "just about us" and thus avoid imposing our choices on anybody else, the more fluidity we introduce into our households. We can become role models to our families, *not necessarily for making the same food change we have made,* but for taking tender, consistent, quiet care of ourselves.

Our commitment becomes a part of who we are to our families. It becomes part of what our family members think can be achieved for themselves, and it expands their own power of choice. It becomes part of their idea of women, of ways women can achieve both independence and belonging. And it's a very strong statement in society today to see a woman at ease with her food. A woman at ease with her food is at ease with many other things.

Points of Depression
Often just when our family dynamic is beginning to settle down on the food issue and we see that we can make our change, something happens. Just as our family accepts our commitment to a new way of eating, reconciles itself to it, often thrives on it, we find

ourselves back in our own internal conflict. We've made our commitment, gotten support, gone through a process with our families, and then our resolve begins to buckle. What is this about?

There are all sorts of psychological interpretations for why we may slump or even reverse ourselves at this point. Having removed all the roadblocks, we may actually feel disappointed that those roadblocks are gone. Sometimes a certain rebellion or forgetfulness about why we wanted this change creeps in. And sometimes we just get depressed. Some women give up everything at this point, even though all the identified blocks have been overcome. They have no answer for why they went back to the old habit. They feel truly defeated. "Take your life in your own hands and what happens?" wrote Erica Jong. "A terrible thing: no one to blame."

Playing in the Dark

I think all of us could spend hours in a therapist's office figuring out what makes us regress in the face of healthy change. (And I wouldn't hesitate to do that, in order to get past a block.) What I think needs to happen at this point is something equivalent to what I call "playing in the dark."

My brother taught music for a number of years in a small Wisconsin town. Many of the children he taught were poor, without much hope or expectation for their lives. My brother met people who were not open to new ideas, who were judgmental, suspicious, and negative. To bring their children in touch with art or imagination or hope was quixotic at best. Still he wanted to expand their world through the music he taught. Every so often, a child would respond in some small way and he would see a glimmer of epiphany.

At the end of the school year the annual concert was held. The students dressed in their best and came excited to play. Parents and townspeople provided an audience. Bravely the children began their program.

One year, the power went out suddenly in the middle of the concert! No electricity, no lights, no way for the children to see their teacher or the music in front of them. And then a miracle happened.

The children played on. Imagine seeing these children—who were so reluctant to believe that anything was possible—playing in the dark. Without premeditation they acted on a faith in themselves to keep going, even when they could not see the music or their teacher or their audience. It showed the children that perhaps they weren't dependent on their surroundings after all. And it showed them that perhaps their surroundings did not dictate every facet of their lives. Maybe they had things inside of them that would prevail—a vision, a knowledge that could not be seen and yet could be experienced, if they just had the courage to play on.

When we have feelings of despair and hopelessness, we are trapped in a way that sometimes we ourselves cannot understand. And the trick of maintaining our change is the trick of playing in the dark. Even when we can't see through our depression, don't know what is happening and why; even when we can't feel our supports; even when we think we are unworthy and have no ability to change; still we play our music. We just keep going, note by note and line by line, until we can see the light again.

This means that we practice our change without feeling at that moment any deep commitment. We do it without liking it. We do it without particularly remembering why we're doing it. Sometimes all those lights go out and we must play on, just doing what we know to do, just doing it by rote. We do it without enthusiasm, without spark, without *energy*. But we do it!

The lights always do come on again, and we get the old enthusiasm and commitment and clarity back. Then we know the darkness is not a sign that we should give up changing. The darkness is a natural part of the cycle of all things, including change. The darkness shows us that the change can go on without any gurus or teachers, without any props of attitude or disposition to bolster it up. We can get through any dark cycle by simply keeping on, by simply practicing what we know even while we acknowledge what we don't know. That's how we find out that, after all, what we know is enough.

The Work of Faith

At points of despair it's helpful for me to remember that I have done the necessary work, the work of faith, in making the commitment to continue on no matter what. Where the work of faith leaves off, Providence takes over. And when the lights come back on and I am no longer in the dark phase of change, I will see more than ever before what the change means to me and how it has expanded my life. When I doubt this, I can go to a living, breathing reminder of it in my own home: my rubber plant.

I have a rubber plant that was very tall and spindly. Healthy enough, it was never very balanced. It only had one branch, its main stalk, and the few leaves extended out from there. Your basic telephone pole.

I'd grown the plant from a seedling and was glad it had survived. Yet I never liked the looks of it and felt frustrated that it continued to live but not to thrive. I considered throwing it out. But before I did, I took a deep breath and tried an experiment. I cut the plant all the way down to the very first leaf.

Lo and behold. The plant soon began to sprout a multitude of branches. Now it is lush and rounded and balanced. I can't get over the miracle of a plant's ability to sprout out. I had done nothing but cut, and everything else was life working its miracle.

This reminds me about the work of faith. I can't know what will happen after I make a change, cut something out, start again at the beginning. I get afraid of the emptiness of being without my habit. If I cut this, what will be left of me? Will I be "stumped"?

The work of faith is very simple. The action is to do away with the thing that weighs me down and start at the beginning, to make a commitment and cut down the skinny stalk of habit or traditional expectation. The action is simple but the fear is complex.

The divinity of life gives us 90 percent for our every 10 percent; it sprouts all kinds of avenues, pathways, branches to replace the single one that was cut. It multiplies our options a hundred times when we let go of the only one we thought would work for us.

Often when I make a change, I think I have to figure this all out in advance. I think *I* am responsible for creating all the alternative branches that will sprout from a single cut stem. But I can no more see all the alternatives to my habit than I can make my plant proliferate. And I don't have to. All I have to do is cut the stem and let go of the one skinny stalk of habit that I think is keeping me alive, or anchoring me, or tying me to those around me.

Then I begin to get a sense of the depth and breadth of the root system below me. Then I see the narrow linear path of what I thought were my options in life sprout a hundred buds of possibility before my eyes. I find out what I'm capable of, what those around me are capable of, what my place in my family really is, how and why I am valued by others, how and why I value myself.

Only then do I realize my own surprise: in spite of years of cultivating faith, I never really expect any help with my growth. In spite of my belief in an interactive God, I tend to think I'm exchanging one tall skinny reed for a stump, because that is all I have power to do. Instead, I exchange one skinny reed for branch after shoot after bud of balance and option.

The Next Layer

Every time I or people around me make a significant change and I see this kind of growth in response, it makes me, as my five-year-old says, "all shiverly!" What more do we dare to do? What other calls do we dare act upon?

When I heed a call to make a change, commit to it, walk through the process, and once again settle in to a new habit, by and by I begin to hear another call. No matter how deeply I go, after a time another layer of change always seems to beckon. When these calls to change are about food, they always end up expanding my life in many ways that have nothing to do with food.

My Own Next Layer: Speed Eating

My most current inner directive has to do with what I call "speed eating." I've always been a speed eater. I can guess why that is. Mealtime was torture growing up, so there was every reason to want to be done with it. Today I have a busy, demanding life, as many of us do, in which taking extra time for *anything* can strike a drum-beating panic in me. In my case, taking my time with food is also connected to a question of entitlement.

I think the feeling that I'm not entitled to food is involved because I remember so vividly the first time I deliberately tried to slow down my food intake. I was barely in my teens. Every meal included dessert in our home, and when we had cookies, our quota was two cookies per person.

I decided one night that I wanted to eat my first cookie slowly and really savor it. I remember wondering: *if I eat this chocolate chip cookie slowly and really pay attention, will just one cookie satisfy me?* So I let each bite melt in my mouth like a communion wafer. I ate around each chocolate chip as I came to it, then finally let myself have the chip, working it through my tongue until the chocolate coated my mouth. This was the taste of cashmere! I still remember everything about the experience, the sight, sound, sensation. When I'd finally finished the cookie, well, it seemed to me that any experience so good ought to be repeated.

But when I reached to the plate for a second cookie, I abruptly got the hook. My father's voice tore into me, "How many cookies have you *had* now!" "One," I squeaked, instantly and utterly shamed. "Well, it certainly seems to me you've been sitting there eating cookies a long time," he said, victoriously catching me in what he thought was an obvious lie.

My family sat and watched me, and no one came to my defense. Silently, defiantly I reached for the second helping to which I was entitled. I gobbled the cookie I certainly now preferred to any of *them,* never looked up, never tasted a thing.

I realize now that I haven't tasted food much of my life. The more aware of this I am, the less comfortable I am, and the more of a loss it seems.

Fondue was a very popular meal in the 1970s, and one night my partner and I made fondue with his sister and her boyfriend. One type of fondue is a hot sauce made of melted cheese and wine, often with eggs, butter, and milk, and often eaten with bread. To make fondue, you put small pieces of bread on sticks like shish kebab and steep them in the hot sauce before eating.

How different it was from a normal meal, because we all had to eat a few bites at a time with significant pauses in between. It was a dinner-long version of sitting around the campfire toasting marshmallows. Once a chunk of food was cooked and ready to be eaten, we savored the mouthful, and we waited patiently for the next bite to be done while we enjoyed each other's company. Supper lasted two or three hours. At the end I noticed that I had eaten less, yet felt unusually satisfied.

I thought, *this is the most deeply civilized meal I've ever had.* Twenty years later the vividness of the memory still calls to me, representing deeper meaning and desire: to make every bite significant, to be completely present at the table.

My Resistance to Slowing Down

This inner directive to eat slowly battles with significant resistance. One resistance comes from our culture, which is hardly geared toward fondue-style eating! Fast food is not just the norm, but a symbol of the pace our society has taken on. When I was in school, students were given about twenty minutes for lunch *and* recess combined. The sooner we ate, the sooner we played; so school taught me to eat faster and faster. My adult attitude stems from the kid who can't wait to get out on the playground: let's get the meal over with so we can go on to do all the millions of pressing, more important things. My children have a similar lunch-and-recess schedule at their school, and they, too, are rewarded for bolting their food.

Apart from cultural resistance, I have a more personal fight within me: that the scene with my father and the cookies will repeat itself. Every time I slow down my eating, a part of me becomes anxious. I'm waiting for someone to bellow, "I can't believe you're *still eating!* How much have you had, anyway? You're lying; it's more! You're not entitled to it! You need that food like a hole in the head!" I expect the recurring specter to shame me with the same words meal after meal, as I am driven back into food compulsion fast and clean like a hammered nail. So I eat—quick—before anyone notices what or how much.

My calling is for a healing counterforce to slow down my food intake. Approaching food slowly gives me the chance to tell myself that I'm entitled to the food I have, that I need it, deserve it, that it's appropriate and important to feed myself.

One way I've worked on slowing down my eating is by sorting out what it is I really have to do to change, what I will have to do less in order to make more time for eating. I also want to eat with people who approach their food with awareness, especially those living in family situations like mine, to see how they do it.

Making My Change within the Family Structure

I am concerned about how eating slowly would change the dynamic within my speed-eating family. I fear lagging behind at the table. I imagine my children sitting bored, picking fights, infuriating my husband as they go wild waiting for the meal to end. Or I imagine my husband eating all the food and leaving nothing for me, or everyone getting up and leaving while I am barely halfway through my meal.

Then I remember the work of faith: I'm only responsible for making the commitment. The changes that will issue from it, what it will look like once I cut down my skinny stalk of habit—all those branches and shoots and buds that I know will issue from it—are not the changes I can make. Those are the changes that will be made for me, once I make the commitment.

Your Own Next Layer

You likely will have your own next layer, whatever the food change you're making now. We can choose to heed call after call, or we can stop with a single change. It's up to each of us. The deeper we go, the more profound the meanings of the changes we make. The more we allow these changes to inform and transform other parts of our lives, the greater the rewards. The more in contact we are with our own bodies, the more we feed ourselves physically and spiritually. The more we feed ourselves well, the more we become who we are.

CHAPTER 5

True Sustenance

Feeding Our Vision

Through the process of changing my food, I've come to believe that inside us is the vision of everything we need to become. This is not to be confused with society's ideal of the perfect us, that boundlessly energetic superwoman who eats perfectly all the time, has the perfect slender body to prove it, has a high-powered fulfilling job, and takes care of her family unstintingly with plenty of energy to spare. That's no vision—that's a nightmare! Trying to live up to that kind of "vision" is like trying to be the perfect guest in our own lives.

Or to use another comparison: trying to conform to society's ideal is like squeezing ourselves into high heels, shoes too "ideal" and Sunday-best to ever move around in. Who among us hasn't bought a pair like that, thinking we'd bought ourselves a heightened glamour, and who among us couldn't wait to get out of those shoes?

More like bare feet, my real, unfolding vision of who and what I want to become isn't very proper. It's without much modesty or orderliness or constraint. Though I never know or "see" this vision in its entirety, its presence can be felt at the core of my soul, waking and sleeping, insistent and persistent and grand. When I sit in prayer and meditation and wonder who I am and what my purpose is, I'm asking for the help to go beyond my fears and bad habits and keep moving toward that vision of what is intended for me. When I am feeling more fearful or lazy and would rather limit than expand myself, I don't want to see any vision. Yet the vision is always there, even when I choose not to acknowledge its callings and even when I answer that I'm incapable.

Remember Who You Are

I think shrugging off our vision of ourselves is a way to deny our godliness. The Disney movie *The Lion King* beautifully illustrates this. In the film the young lion Simba is driven through shame into self-exile. He adopts an attitude of spiritual nonchalance and leads a reduced life that has little to do with his real purpose. He runs away from his own royalty, his own "godliness" if you will. He uses his guilt as the reason to avoid living the life he is called to live. "I'm not worthy," he says to himself.

Who among us has not said that to ourselves in the face of our own vision? Because our vision is immodest, royal, and larger than the lives we back ourselves into, we say we can't live up to its potential. Or maybe we could have achieved this or that, taken this or that risk, made this or that change when we were younger, but the time has passed.

In *The Lion King*, Simba changes when his father appears to him in a vision and thunders, "Remember who you are." A friend of mine who's struggling to change her compulsive relationship with food bought a Lion King shower curtain bordered with the words *Remember who you are.* She uses it as a reminder of her own vision. It's one way she brings to her daily routine the imagination and play needed to bring a vision to life. The image on the shower curtain invites her to do more than scrub her body automatically and get it over with. It invites her to strip herself of the outside trappings, clean herself of all the residual dirt that keeps her from making good changes, and make for herself a baptism. She has made something as mundane as a shower curtain into a personal amulet. She uses it to remember who she is and who she is called to be.

I need my amulets too. When my family surrounds me at Halloween with their thick chocolate breath, when they eat huge late dinners, when they pile on the food at holidays, when we're on vacation and they chow down meal after meal of food I love but know I cannot eat, I need to remember who I am. I love my family but I am not them; kin but not necessarily akin. Continually I have to find ways to be with them and still honor who I am.

Honoring Our Uniqueness

When we move toward our vision, we honor our "royalty" or godliness, our uniqueness, our potential, and our equally crucial gifts of limitation. We will claim the very characteristics that set us apart from others, even from those closest to us in life. Our vision for ourselves is uniquely our own and surprisingly private. Our spouses, friends, and family likely know when we practice a habit that goes against this vision because it makes us miserable. They also know some things we feel good about and some things about who we wanted and still want to become. But they never know everything. We ourselves aren't conscious of everything. Yet the more aware we are of our own vision, the more room, imagination, and play we give that vision, the more it unfolds. We fumble and slide and sometimes back away; but when we want peace, we find ourselves moving toward the person we want to be, were meant to be. Then we move closer toward our personal Maker of vision; we make a constant progression toward God.

"Narcissism breaking up invites us to expand the boundaries of who we think we are," wrote Thomas Moore in his book *Care of the Soul.* A great example of narcissism in action is the self-absorption of berating ourselves about our eating. When we're busy chastising ourselves, we can't really pay attention to anything or anyone else. Nourishing ourselves in a way that honors our bodies takes us out of that self-absorption—it's "narcissism breaking up." When we grow comfortable with our food being different from other people's food, when we become comfortable with a different role of food provider from the one we thought we had to play, we expand the boundaries. The paradox is that the truer we are to that inner vision of who and what we are intended to be, the less self-obsessed and freer of ego we are.

Silence and Solitude

The most nourishing foods I know for feeding the vision of self, that vision of expanded boundaries, are silence and solitude. If I am to hear the still small voice within that remembers who I am, I must be alone and quiet every day. This is because in the face of temptation, tradition, inner and outer resistance, I need to keep making choices that support my change.

Clearing the Space

The leaders at a retreat I was recently on explained how the forest land on which the retreat center was built was given to them. They had wanted some grass around the new retreat center building, so they consulted the state's Department of Natural Resources to find out how best to make a lawn without disturbing the surrounding forest lands. The foresters said all they needed to do was clear away the land around the building. The grass seeds were already buried within the soil, they said, waiting for the right conditions. Once the land was cleared, the grass would come on its own.

So it is with our lives. An inner directive to change is a divinely placed seed, waiting for the right conditions. Our responsibility is to "clear away the land," provide the silence and solitude, the space within our lives, to enable the seed to grow. Then when all the old messages crowd in—"I have no time for this. It's too hard. My family doesn't like it. I hate eating differently from others. I miss my old habits. They're all eating this so why can't I?"—this seed of change is given enough room to sprout, if just to carry a single message, "Do it anyway."

The Pilot Light

Many days I enter into quiet time with no particular spiritual feeling, just looking for a way to rest my senses. I close my eyes, sit up or lie down, breathe deeply, and consciously relax my muscles. Before long I find myself focusing within, entering a hypnotic state that I think of as "staring into the pilot light."

A pilot light keeps burning in a stove whether the heat is on or off. A pilot light burns within the human soul as well, waiting for us to call upon that power. And whether we're "on," spiritually connected and aware, or "off," isolated and unaware, the pilot light keeps burning.

Quiet time gives me the opportunity to recognize my very being, struggles and all, as sacred. It reminds me that a miracle occurred just so that I could be alive and come into this world, one of a kind. It reminds me that the pilot light still burns within me, giving my heart the power to keep beating.

That reminder helps me with all kinds of individuality issues—how I am alike, yet different, from those in my world. I clear away the details of my life enough to remember and arrange a small experience with the life force of my soul, the only soul I am bound to honor, the commitment that supersedes all other commitments.

This can be a powerful understanding for us as women with families. If we are to claim our individuality with food or anything else, we need to give ourselves this time and space to learn and remember and relearn and reremember this. We can experience wonderful moments of love, insight, and connectedness with family, with friends, at church or synagogue, in our neighborhoods, at work. But those moments don't give us the commitment to our bodies that lasting food change requires. Silence and solitude give us that sustenance, because they provide undiluted opportunities to stare into our own pilot light and experience ourselves.

Finding the Time

How do we women with families find silence and solitude, these rarest of rare commodities? Take silence, for instance. From airplane noise to traffic noise to TV talk shows to talk radio, life itself is getting increasingly noisy for all of us. Add to that the typical scenes of family life: the oldest child is panicking about an overdue homework assignment while the youngest is bellowing for supper, and the spouse is complaining about work and the telephone is ringing while the plumber is waiting to be paid though the toilet's still leaking, when just then the doorbell rings and what kind of Girl Scout cookies would we like to order? ("Oh, all of them.") Noise, especially human noise, is the fabric of our lives, and silence has little natural place unless it's 2 A.M. or unless we become committed to getting some.

Solitude is no easier to come by and no more valued in our culture. "What a commentary on our civilization," wrote Anne Morrow Lindbergh, "when being alone is considered suspect; when one has to apologize for it, make excuses, hide the fact that one practices it—like a secret vice!" There is supposed to be something sad and terrible about eating alone, going to movies alone, vacationing alone: a sign of failure. It took my partner a long time to understand that I have a real need for solitude. He has come to accept it because, time after time, he sees me enter into solitude dark and depleted, and emerge from it as though I'd warmed myself by a fire on a cold winter day, relaxed in my bones.

I find silence and solitude by getting up earlier than the rest of my family. Since I work full time, I make sure most of my lunch hours contain at least some quiet. I'm constantly looking at the day's or weekend's family schedule, sniffing out possibilities for a bit of quiet time. When I find it, I write "S & S" on the calendar and openly stake my claim on the time block. If my family trespasses onto my time, I become a good animal protecting my turf and baring my incisors.

Even the smallest amount of "S & S" during the day can help. I've been known to pull over to the side of the road before I get to daycare to pick up my children at the end of the day. There I give myself five minutes' worth of laying my head on the steering wheel and breathing in and out, feeling my blood in my veins and inwardly staring into my pilot light.

I also schedule longer periods of time for silence and solitude. I promise myself a weekend getaway once every season, four times a year, of doing something as light as house-sitting or as serious as a structured retreat. So my husband and children practice being without me for short but consistent amounts of time. I give my spouse at least an equal amount of time for his own getaways, for his own purposes, so there is equity and cooperation all around.

What Holds Us Back

Say you decide that you, too, want some of this silence and solitude. But something holds you back. You may be afraid of what your partner will say or do. You may wonder whether your family can be without you. All that may be difficult, but you admit you could probably work something out if you were really committed to it. Perhaps you take steps in this direction and then find underneath it another, deeper fear—the fear of getting what you're asking for.

We may fear that once we really get full and regular helpings of freedom from the bottomless responsibilities of wife and mother, we will find ourselves insatiable—we'll be led further and further away until we never want to come back. We may wonder secretly if we'll turn into a version of the converted feminist housewife of the early seventies, who scrubbed one too many floors, cooked one too many casseroles, and suddenly hopped on the back of someone's motorcycle and was never heard from again.

However this fantasy plays out, the fear behind it is very real and born of what women are asked to be and to do. We can sacrifice so much of ourselves for so long in the effort to be the "good" mother, the "good" partner, that we wonder what will happen the day we dig in our heels and say *enough*. Our inner pendulum could swing like the heroine Eva's did in Tillie Olsen's story *Tell Me a Riddle*. After a lifetime of duty to her family, Eva refused to go with her husband into a retirement community: "She would not exchange her solitude for anything. *Never again to be forced to move to the rhythm of others."* (Olsen's italics.)

Yet like so many of our fears about taking an independent road with food, this fear almost always proves unfounded. We do become satiated with alone time once we have the space to remember why we chose to live with others. Sometimes we need to be without them to remember where our family ends and we begin. Declaring our independence in this way, like declaring our independence with food, does not take us away from the family after all. It gives our family members time to reconsider us and our contributions, our needs separate from them. It redefines our place in the family as someone far more dimensional than "she who gives."

Redefining Our Place as Food Provider

Once we have found the right food to feed ourselves in body and spirit and have given ourselves the silence and the solitude to maintain our change, often we find ourselves refashioning our traditional role as food provider in order to maintain our own change. Like our food covenants, we may only realize the rules we had about feeding others when we start to break those rules.

Cutting Out the Labels

We all have labels, definitions, and instructions about what it means to provide food for our family. Here are some labels we may use:

- I should eat the way I was raised.
- The way to a man's heart is through his stomach.
- I, as the woman of the house, need to be the embodiment of hearth and home.

• A responsible mother and partner does not cause family disruption or place her own needs first.

Labels can be useful instructions, guides to what a role means in life and how to go about filling it. But when we make a change, particularly one as potentially powerful as a significant food change, these labels may no longer serve us.

I was reminded of this not long ago, when I realized I could get rid of the labels in my leotards. I've exercised for many years, so I've acquired a few leotards for aerobics classes. Exercise clothes make up for their lack of flattery (at least a little!) by their soft breathing comfort on the body. The labels in my leotards felt especially stiff and crinkly because they contrasted sharply with the softness of the fabric.

For the longest time, the labels in my leotards bothered me. They poked out on a regular basis, whenever they weren't jutting stiff against my skin. But the labels came with the clothes and it didn't occur to me that I could do anything other than live with them. Finally, one day I realized I didn't need to live with them, and I hunted up a scissors. I cut the labels out slowly, carefully, so I wouldn't accidentally nick the fabric. Then out they came and I was free of them.

I think something similar happens to us when we redefine our place as food provider. We see that we can't provide food with the same old idea, "I'll make all our food, we'll all eat the same thing together, and that makes for one big happy family." We can't do what our mothers or grandmothers did, whether these ideas succeeded for them or not. So we look at our old labels of what it means to be a partner and a mother.

Any labels that no longer fit our vision of ourselves begin to scrape against us. We tuck them underneath our consciousness and they poke out again. They feel stiff and inflexible. Gradually we become more and more aware of how uncomfortable those labels are, until they absolutely hurt.

Then we decide to get the scissors. We cut slowly and mindfully through each part of the paradigm that doesn't work for us. We cut with care, knowing that the scissors is powerful, that it has the power to cut through the whole fabric of our lives. We take our time, cutting a little at a time. We pay attention.

And when the label is gone, we are free to be an original. So *we* decide when and how and whether we will cook meals; *we* decide whether we need to eat our food separately or together with our family. *We* decide if we want to cook someone else's meat if we're vegetarian, prepare someone else's dessert if we don't eat it, or make someone else's coffee if we've quit drinking it. *We* decide whether we want to provide meals at all and, if so, which ones, and what the alternatives are to our providing meals. In the process of changing our food we discover that we redefine our place as food provider into one that reflects the place of food in our lives. We become comfortable once more or maybe for the first time. Eventually that comfort spills over and is felt by, and reflected by, the rest of our family.

The Soft Overcomes the Hard

A book of wise spiritual teachings, the classic *Tao Te Ching,* says, "The soft overcomes the hard; the gentle overcomes the rigid." The Tao uses water as an example: Water washes over whatever it touches in softness and fluidity. But in the end, water wears down rocks, cement, diamonds—the densest and hardest of materials.

When I remember and flow with the power of this softness, there is no need to demand that my family get "in line," no need that my friends get "on board." Lecturing myself or anybody else about my food change or their own food habits becomes absurd. That's the brittleness of a New Year's resolution, of evangelizing to try to convince myself. I am most at peace when I can hold my peace, bending into the frequent chaos of family life and work life.

I thought about this recently when a fierce summer storm hit our area. It was late afternoon and my family hadn't come home yet. I was restless and driven in my tasks, eager to make the most of the time I had to myself. But then I was moved to put aside everything I was doing and watch the storm. The wilder the storm became, the quieter I became inwardly, as though nature had effortlessly tossed up all my free-floating agitation and blew it away. The power lines went down and the sky turned grayish-green. Winds sent tree branches crashing on our roof and rain fell like knives across our lawn.

I watched a little tree in our front yard bend over in every direction. Lightning and gale were splitting the giant oaks along our street. I thought surely this treelet would not survive.

But at the end it was standing, minus some leaves but little worse for wear. It survived because it became one with the storm; it could bend in whatever direction the wind took it, because it was so supple. The tree's gift to me was a study in adaptability. It was "the soft overcoming the hard" made visible.

When I remember this lesson, I am at peace with my choices in the midst of the frequent chaos of family life and work life. My goal is not to cling to my commitment in the white-knuckle sense, like an object standing stiff in order to prevail against the winds. My goal is to become my change as much as I can, as the little tree became part of whatever surrounded it.

How does all this translate into my family life? If my family members need to eat at separate times, I help them do it when I can. If for whatever reason I can't tolerate their food around me, I have them get it themselves or have my husband get it for our children and remove myself from the kitchen. I accommodate what they need as I ask them to accommodate me. If family members or friends are making consistent food choices I "know" are bad for them, I strive to keep my silence and leaven that silence with compassion when I see them struggle, just as I want compassion for myself. If there is a big family sit-down dinner at holiday time, I'm most content when I make a plan ahead of time to modify my food intake and mealtimes to accommodate the dinner. During holidays I continue to bypass foods that don't work for me, without making any particular issue of it to others. I work on responding without defensiveness when someone else makes a fuss about what I'm eating or not eating.

When I put into practice the phrase "The soft overcomes the hard," I realize that resisting any of these situations is "the hard." Thinking that I need to educate other people is "the hard." Judging myself is "the hard." Judging others is "the hard." Fear that I can't survive with my food choices in a certain situation, fear that I will break in a gale of temptation is "the hard." Fear itself is "the hard."

Not that I don't feel fear. I do. But the process of feeding others what I cannot eat is the process of choosing love over fear. I feel both—not consciously, not all the time, but love and fear are there. I can still feel desire to have the food others are having. I can still feel jealous when I know I can't have what they're having without damaging myself. I still want to join them at times.

Often for me the soft way, the way of love, the way of saying yes to whatever is going on, is the way of least action—least action not just with others, but also with myself. For instance, I move through temptation best when I'm willing to sit with the racy feeling within. I'll probably learn something when I sit with it, and the feeling, like any feeling, will sooner or later go away. But to fight temptation is to adopt a brittle attitude that can snap in a storm. Rather, I observe my temptations as they happen, while striving to *become* my change, like the little tree stayed intact by becoming one with the storm. Then I don't need to fight for it any more than I fight for my hazel eyes or dimples. Practicing my change is just a part of remembering who I am and who I am becoming.

This means there are days when I can make my husband and children their food and it's perfectly fine that I don't eat along with them. Or I can sit with them while they eat, even though it isn't my time for a meal. But other times, I may feel jealous, deprived, self-pitying about the food they're eating that I'm not. Then I find another means of getting them fed while I do something else.

Because I want understanding and consideration from my family members about my decisions, I try to give the same to them. My husband usually prepares his own food and I don't comment on his choices. I don't try to force either my husband or my children into meals. I take very seriously the cues from my family about what and when they want to eat. I don't bully my children into eating that last little bit of something on the plate or my husband into finishing leftovers before they spoil. This isn't always easy because I hate throwing food away. So we strive for a balance: my goal is to honor their choices, and in turn they try to be sensitive to the fact that food is important to me.

Feeding Others

Recognizing my own soul issues surrounding food has made me more aware of my desire to feed people beyond my own family. It seems ironic that, on the one hand, I am led to loosen my hold on the role of food provider within the family, but on the other hand, I've become more committed to feeding others.

As a compulsive person, I spent most of my life trying to get enough. But in my frantic efforts to satisfy myself, I ate far more than my share. To address the abuses of my past, I have made food-shelf shopping a regular part of my grocery shopping ritual. Giving to the food shelves has given me new sparks of connectedness with others. When my children were newborns, I took special pleasure in donating infant formula. Around the holidays, I love to donate holiday food. I know food stamps don't cover toiletries, so donating toothpaste when I go to the dentist or body lotion when my skin gets chapped in winter brings an added dimension to my life. Our family is on a food budget, but I afford the food-shelf shopping by clipping coupons; whatever money I save from them becomes my food-shelf allowance for the week. I say "thank you" for the divine help I've received by making a small contribution toward somebody else's well-being.

Some people who make food changes ransack their kitchen for all traces of the foods or beverages they've quit and donate them to the food shelves. Other people want to give only those things they can eat in peace now. My children like to give their favorite foods so they don't envision adding to the burden of other children—"Oh the poor poor!"—by giving them things like canned asparagus. They like to choose what they give, and they like to put the items in the food-shelf collection bins themselves.

These weekly rituals are meaningful to my family because our giving is personal. The more personal it is, the more soulful—and for me, the more healing.

Mutuality

It's the very personal nature of giving that creates a sense of mutuality—the sense that I am giving, yet I am abundantly receiving.

At its best, the essence of family life is mutuality. Families walk through large parts of life side by side, parents and children alike attempting the hard work of growing up. And "up" is the word, because many days it is an uphill climb. But it is a stairway to heaven.

It's a stairway to heaven because *mutual* is not *reciprocal*. Both words connote give and take, but reciprocal is a much more literal, tit-for-tat exchange: "I did this for you; now you owe me that." Yet we don't love equally at the same times; we don't give or provide in the same ways. The failure of reciprocity to satisfy in family life may be best illustrated where it's ultimately practiced: in divorce. Once we enter into the divorce process, all of life is reduced to "I'll take this; you take that. I'll concede on this point only if I can get that." And in the end, everyone feels cheated.

Mutuality speaks to something different. Mutuality doesn't directly compare what I owe you and what you owe me. It's closeness without sameness and compares on only one level: an intangible, purely subjective bottom line. Mutuality is achieved when both know that they got what they needed; that whether in ease or in difficulty, the connection was all worth it. And we know for certain the other person's needs were me too.

When we hold our newborn baby in our arms and feed it, it's a time of pure mutuality, even though it may appear from the outside that we are the ones doing all the giving. Being needed so absolutely evokes our own absolute need for our baby. The desire to nurture this baby feels euphoric because it puts us in constant touch with the part of us that is overwhelming, simple, unconditional love. We want to go on feeling this love we never knew we were capable of, and we can only feel that through giving to the child. And so the need is truly mutual right from the beginning. How quickly and frequently thereafter the tables keep turning between parent and child, on who needs whom!

When mutuality is at work within a family, everybody in the family knows it. Even though children do much of the taking and parents much of the giving, children have the gift of knowing they add to their parents' lives in essential ways. Parents openly show their children that they anchor and expand them, allowing mutuality to happen. Partners likewise know each gets what they need, though they may not "do" for each other in reciprocal senses.

New Currency of Exchange

This concept of mutuality has become very important to me as I've honored my commitments with food. It's harder for other people to make me food when I eat differently from them, and those who want to establish connection with me through food have been frustrated at times. So I've looked for new ways to get that special feeling of exchange.

I was comparing notes with a friend on this topic recently, and our conversation drifted to our mothers' adjustments to our food changes through the years. It used to be that our mothers sent all kinds of leftover food home with us whenever we were invited to dinner. But since we stopped eating many of the things our mothers cooked, slowly both of our mothers began giving us magazines they had finished reading. As we talked, my friend and I suddenly recognized that we were receiving a different form of "leftovers"! We read into the gesture that our mothers had accepted our food changes. And we both enjoy being treated with the magazines. We know our mothers still want to give to us, and we, as grown children, still want to show our need and appreciation of our mothers' pivotal place in our lives. So magazines have become a new source of exchange between mother and daughter.

Since I don't eat the same as many other people, I try to stay attuned for other currency of exchange like the magazines, and I work to bring that into my life to strengthen the ties between me and those I love. But as with the magazines, mutuality often finds its own expression without any help from me.

Lighting the Candle
One way I have strengthened the mealtime ties between my children and me has been to start a ritual of lighting a candle at the breakfast table.

Nearly every special occasion meal of my childhood was a candle-lit one. There were also periods of time when candles were a part of my life. Once when my mother went through a difficult time, she started lighting candles at our suppers and made old wine bottles into works of art by melting rainbows of colored wax on them. My grandmother also lit candles at the meal table. When she invited me for meals, there was something lovely and important about her lighting a candle for just the two of us.

I remember these things as my children and I eat breakfast by candlelight. I used to read the newspaper at breakfast while they watched TV. But since I've been lighting the candle, we frequently put away our diversions to gather together with our food around the candle.

Lighting a candle sets me firmly on the ground of gratitude. It anchors me in those times and places when I was fed lovingly and well. It evokes a sacred feeling for me that has been important in helping me make food changes. It reminds me of places of worship, of burning autumn leaves, of the winter hearth, of bringing light into darkness.

I light the candle for the goodness of those times and traditions. I light the candle in the hopes of passing this flame on to my family members when they think back on how I have fed them.

Lighting a candle has become one way to restructure my food triangle, a means of establishing connection to my family without eating the same food. When I create little rituals like this, I find I can eat differently from my husband and children and yet feel more profoundly connected to them than I would if I were eating the same. "These two—community and individuality—go together," wrote Thomas Moore in *Soul Mates*. "You can't have a genuine community unless it consists of true individuals, and you can't be an individual unless you are deeply involved in community."

Communion

Like lighting a candle, communion is one of my childhood rituals that has not just evolved in meaning for me but has metamorphosed into something alike yet completely different from my original experience. In the symbolism of communion I find all that I want my food and the eating experience with others to be.

The Christian service or Mass culminates in communion. Taking place at the very end of worship, communion is presented as the ultimate union. It's the sacred center of the church service, what everything before it leads up to, the crescendo of interaction with God and with each other. It's the ultimate rite to put us to rights.

Communion recognizes that, perhaps second only to lovemaking, no human activity is as bonding and intimate as sharing a significant meal. In a church service it's the central act of reconciliation and wholeness.

The prayer and ritual and readings from sacred texts that come before communion lead us to this central act. For me, all the changes I have made and the ways I have come to terms with my food lead me to communion, this participation of food with my family members. Being able to eat alongside them, at peace with them and they with me, is true communion. It is ordinary life and also *extraordinary*, a sacrament, a visible form of invisible grace.

Grace

Many people have the custom of saying grace, the short prayer of blessing and thanksgiving, before meals. Saying grace could also be viewed as a miniaturized version of a worship service, collapsing all that comes before communion into one small prayer. In our house, grace currently goes like this: "We wish for peace, happiness, and food for all the people around the world. Amen." I like this simple prayer because it's such a bald declaration of need.

As a family unit, we share one another's needs. This is true whether we want to, realize it, or intend to. One of the toughest aspects of living with others is that we not only have to cope with all the ways we ourselves are burdened and unreconciled, but we inevitably cope with the confusion and darkness inside our loved ones too. The form of grace I say with my family is a declaration that in our separate searches for the peace, happiness, and food we yearn for, we are all in this together.

In this prayer of grace we are also reaffirming knowledge of the human struggle, extending far beyond our little family unit. We're committing ourselves to something larger than we are: the peace, happiness, and food of others. With these words, we acknowledge the spiritual link between "them" and "us," so that we may break down the barriers and break bread with everyone.

I like to visualize that "saying grace" is calling the state of grace to me. When I am in the state of grace, there is no agenda I need to push, no task, attitude, or feeling I require from myself or anyone else. I move through difficulties in an effortless way. I am moved by the wisdom of the people around me even while I know the same wisdom is available to me. In the state of grace, the world is rich and wonderful and made for laughter. I am constantly fed.

Starting a meal with grace allows me the image of becoming, for this space of time, one of the lilies of the valley that "toil not, neither do they spin." I can make my independent food choices while embracing the fact that every one of us is, without exception, dependent. Knowing this, I can experience communion with everyone.

And so I enter into this meal, this communion with my family, one of thousands of meals before and I hope, thousands to come. I enter into it evoking the state of grace, for my family and for me. It begins with the wish that we all will be fed just the right amount of what we need. And then we eat.

And that is the great "Amen."

It's almost Christmas. I am five years old. My parents, my brother, and I are making the three-hour pilgrimage to a small town where my grandparents live. We arrive and I fling open their back door, trumpeting, "We're here, we're here! It took so long I thought we would be sick!" The almond scent that saturates their house announces the one, the only, spritz cookies. I race around the corner and there they are, a jubilee on cookie sheets, each one so unique, so perfect, like presents under the tree. I ask my grandmother, "Can we save some for Santa? He's been good too!" She bends down to claim my cheeks with big almond-fragrant hands; my grandfather stands just behind her, tapping his pipe and awaiting his turn; and there is nothing better than this moment.

It's almost Christmas. I am fourteen. My nomadic grandmother has lived in about ninety apartments since Grandpa died, looking for home. I'm in her new place that looks just like the old place, and she hovers over my spritz cookies in her kitchen. "See, the consistency of the dough has to be *just right,* just like this. . . . Maybe you should add a little more flour. . . . The cookie press is tricky, watch, see how I work it. . . . But don't you think the cookies look better decorated this way, dear?" On and on she goes even though I know how to do it for heaven's sake, I've done it a million *times* already! At least I get to bring the cookies home when we're done. Maybe I could sneak some for myself on the way home and shake up the container to make it look full—the old Momster will never be the wiser. I paste alertness on my face as Grandma coaches on, but there's nothing more tedious than this moment.

It's almost Christmas. I've been married a little over a year. I go over to my grandmother's latest apartment to bake spritz cookies. I get her to experiment with making each cookie larger. "The bigger the better," I say. She pouts that it's ruining their shapes. "Well, then, let's eat all the dough. Think how much less trouble this whole thing would be!" I reply. "Oh look Grandma, another cookie broke. Gotta eat it quick and put it out of its misery." Finally we finish baking and clean up the kitchen together. "Destroy the evidence!" she declares as we laugh and wash, conspire and dry. As always, she lets me keep everything we've baked together. I head out the door stuffed full of cookies inside and out, balancing several cookie-filled coffee cans on my expanded stomach ledge. She finds my hand underneath the mounds, squeezes it, and says, "Don't make a stranger of yourself." I huff, "What, I can't wear my Groucho glasses to dinner Thursday?" She grins into my grin, and there's nothing more filling than this moment.

It's almost Christmas. I am divorced, in therapy, estranged from most of my family, unhappily living with my boyfriend. I call in sick at work to study for my final exam in a difficult class I didn't want to take, for a graduate program I never bargained would accept me. I swallow my fear by thinking, *It's early. I don't need to go to the library yet. I'll work up to it.* I decide to make spritz cookies instead. I have a cold and I can't catch even a whiff of almond, but I don't care. Recklessly I take short cuts, wrestle with the cookie press, gobble dough, undercook the cookies, decorate them assembly-line style, and devour them the same way. It's midafternoon by the time I dress my bloated body in dirty sweatclothes, numb but not numb enough to still the panic of cramming a day's worth of study into forty-five minutes. I grab my car keys and catch myself in the mirror: patches of flour on my face, in my hair, and there is nothing more dreadful than this moment.

It's almost Christmas. It's been seven months since I broke up with my boyfriend, and I am grappling for ways to make it through the Yuletide. My grandmother calls to say she tried making a batch of spritz on her own, but the work was too much for her and she had to lie down. I come over, seat her next to me, pick up the baking where she left off, tell her, "I really couldn't do this without you, my lucky charm!" Bleary and querulous, she skims my work: "I don't see how you expect to bake these cookies and not taste them. How on earth will you know they turned out?" I explain again why I've got to quit eating sweets. I tell her it's okay, I can feel when the dough is right, like reading Braille. She looks unconvinced, betrayed, fragile as yellow parchment. Finally we give up on budging each other's viewpoint and she edges back to bed. The cookies corral me as I clean up her kitchen. *How can I eat them; how can I never eat them?* I muffle the clatter of bowls and pans so I don't disturb her. But it's so quiet, too quiet, and there is nothing bleaker than this moment.

It's almost Christmas. Two years past the loss of my grandmother, there is no end to the loss. I talk my college-age niece into baking spritz cookies with me so we can give them for Christmas presents. Over to her student housing I cart box after box of utensils and ingredients, since her kitchen boasts only the essential beer, chips, can opener, and leftover Burger King from last semester. I bring music, too, wanting our time together to be such a dance that she'll never even notice the sweat. But I'm a poor choreographer today, awkward and irritable, fatigued as only the seven months' pregnant can be. Drudgery balloons while our conversation flattens. I know my niece is struggling with food. Casting for something positive, I seize a cookie and declare it's been two years since I've eaten one of these. "Can you believe it?" I bite my tongue as she glowers and hunches over, looking like she can't wait to be rid of me. *Why are we doing this,* I wonder, and there is nothing lonelier than this moment.

It's almost Christmas, the first Christmas in our new house. My baby, toddler, and husband are all napping at once. *Carpe diem!* In a burst of optimism that this quietude will last, I get out all the makings for spritz cookies. The dough turns out just right, the cookie press cooperates, and with a grateful *whew* I sit down to decorate the pans of artful shapes. Jump back up. Go to the curio cabinet, bring out my grandmother's photograph in the heavy gold frame, take it into the kitchen, and set it next to me on the counter. I don't look at the picture much but feel the heat of her face next to mine all the while I decorate the cookies. I think about telling my mother I did this, knowing she'll think it's absurdly sentimental but knowing I'll tell her anyway, and there is nothing more peaceful than this moment.

It's almost Christmas. "Time to bake the spritz," I announce. My little girl wants to help with enthusiasm twice her size. My boy wanders off, watches football, wanders in, volunteers to decorate a few cookies, says Dad wonders when they can eat them. While I mix ingredients, my daughter waits by dancing to *The Nutcracker.* "Oh no! Fun is being had without me!" I shriek and run to scoop her up. We dance a fanatic twirl in the Land of Snows and settle down again to decorate. She clothes her cookies—and the floor, and Daddy's briefcase, and the insides of her shoes—with giant heaps of colored sugars. She eats stray bits of dough, offers them to me, "Just a little piece, just a candied cherry?" "But *you're* my sweet!" I say and nibble her neck while she giggles on cue. Hours later we finish the cleanup, spent and toasty. This calls for a sprawl on the bean bag chair, and we mash our faces into its cool leather. She lifts her head. "Mama, can we bake spritz cookies again tomorrow?" I claim her cheeks with my almond hands, and there is nothing better than this moment.

Bibliography

Epigraph

Easwaran, Eknath. *God Makes the Rivers to Flow, 13-14* 2d ed. Tomales, Calif.: Blue Mountain Center of Meditation, 1991.

Chapter 1

Hampl, Patricia. Quoted in *Beacon Book of Quotations by Women,* compiled by Rosalie Maggio, 95. Boston: Beacon Press, 1992.

Martin, Judith. Quoted in *Beacon Book of Quotations by Women,* compiled by Rosalie Maggio, 94. Boston: Beacon Press, 1992.

Chapter 2

Estés, Ph.D., Clarissa Pinkola. *Women Who Run with the Wolves, 201–202.* New York: Ballantine Books, 1992. Paraphrased (by Dr. Estés).

von Goethe, Johann. Quoted in *The Artist's Way,* by Julia Cameron, 67. New York: Putnam Publishing Group, 1992.

My Dinner with Andre. Carmel, Calif.: Pacific Arts Video Records, 1982.

Chapter 3

McLaughlin, Mignon. Quoted in *Beacon Book of Quotations by Women,* compiled by Rosalie Maggio, 43. Boston: Beacon Press, 1992.

Hellman, Lillian. Quoted in *Beacon Book of Quotations by Women,* compiled by Rosalie Maggio, 43. Boston: Beacon Press, 1992.

Alther, Lisa. Quoted in *Beacon Book of Quotations by Women,* compiled by Rosalie Maggio, 238. Boston: Beacon Press, 1992.

Nin, Anais. Quoted in *Beacon Book of Quotations by Women,* compiled by Rosalie Maggio, 57. Boston: Beacon Press, 1992.

David, Marc. *Nourishing Wisdom,* 5–6. New York: Bell Tower, 1991.

Davis, Adelle. Quoted in *Beacon Book of Quotations by Women,* compiled by Rosalie Maggio, 94. Boston: Beacon Press, 1992.

Allen, Woody. *Sleeper.* Video CBS Fox, 1984.

Mansfield, Katherine. Quoted in *Beacon Book of Quotations by Women,* compiled by Rosalie Maggio, 120. Boston: Beacon Press, 1992.

Trapp, Maria Augusta. Quoted in *Beacon Book of Quotations by Women,* compiled by Rosalie Maggio, 83. Boston: Beacon Press, 1992.

Saint Teresa of Avila. *Columbia Granger's World of Poetry on CD ROM.* Columbia: Columbia University Press, 1992.

Chapter 4

Menninger, Karl. *The Human Mind,* 3. New York: Alfred A. Knopf, 1964.

Jong, Erica. Quoted in *The Artist's Way,* by Julia Cameron, 74. New York: Putnam Publishing Group, 1992.

Chapter 5

Moore, Thomas. *Care of the Soul,* 63. New York: HarperCollins, 1992.

Lindbergh, Anne Morrow. *Gift from the Sea,* 50. New York: Vintage, 1955.

Olsen, Tillie. *Tell Me a Riddle,* 68. New York: Bantam, Doubleday, Dell Publishing, 1961.

Tzu, Lao. *Tao Te Ching.* Translated by Stephen Mitchell, 78. New York: Harper and Row, 1988.

Moore, Thomas. *Soul Mates,* 233–34. New York: HarperCollins, 1994.

ABOUT THE AUTHOR

Karen Burke has been active in Twelve Step recovery for fourteen years—learning, writing, speaking, and sponsoring. She has a B.A. in pre-law and an M.A. in industrial relations, and works in the field of education and communication. Karen lives in a suburb of Minneapolis with her husband and two young children.